PAX: THE BENEDICTINE WAY

Ambrose Tinsley OSB

Pax:
The Benedictine
Way

A Liturgical Press Book

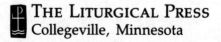

THE LITURGICAL PRESS
Collegeville, Minnesota

This edition published by
THE LITURGICAL PRESS
Collegeville, Minnesota 56321
in association with The Columba Press, Dublin, Ireland

Cover by Bill Bolger
Illustrations by Benedict Tutty OSB
Origination by The Columba Press
Printed in Ireland

ISBN 0-8146-2395-6

Table of Contents

A note on the drawings in this book

Each drawing is on the theme of light and is influenced by Scripture. First there is the story of Creation when God said: 'Let there be light' (Gen 1:3). Then there is the Burning Bush, the symbol of all those who are consumed, but not in any way destroyed, by God's own deifying life (Ex 3:2). The third one shows the Pillar of Fire which guided all those Chosen People on their journey to the Promised Land (Ex 13:21). The fourth is 'Christ the Light' (*cf* Jn 1:12) although that light casts many shadows on our lives. The fifth is Light Invisible (*cf* 1 Tim 6:16) which, though it is reflected to us in so many ways, cannot in itself be ever fully seen.

Introduction

Some years ago I was invited to address a group of people on 'The Benedictine Way'. For them it was to be an extra day within a course on spirituality which they were taking at the time and, as a preparation for my contribution, I made out a list of headings which I thought should be developed in my talks. However, when we all assembled and before I started to elaborate on what I had prepared, I asked the people in that group to make at least a mental list of what they thought I was about to say. That would, I ventured to suggest, help them to see more clearly what ingredients I would be emphasising and, perhaps, which ones I would omit! I hoped that that would make 'The Benedictine Way' (an expression which I much prefer to 'Benedictine Spirituality') more clear. In fact, it turned out to be quite a useful exercise and I decided then that, if I ever had to speak on this same topic to another group, it would be good to recommend that same approach again.

It was about that time, however, that the thought came to my mind that, maybe, it might also be a good idea to write a book and so to share a number of the things I said that day with many other people, too. To do this I decided to attend a meeting in a Benedictine House in England which was to discuss the problems of presenting Benedictinism to the people who come to our monasteries and spend some time as guests. Some of our discussions there, which I found very useful, helped me to reflect a little more on what could be considered as the Christian-essence of the Benedictine Rule and, so, in different ways, they have influenced the content of this book. However, there is one important quality of Benedictine life which got particular attention during

our few days: it is its sensitivity to light and colour, sound and
movement and, although they were not mentioned quite so
much, to perfumes and the very feel of ordinary things.
Appreciation of such sensitivities, I knew, could not be nurtured
by mere words and so, while I was working on this book, I kept
on saying to myself: 'My words are not enough; if this work is to
do what I would have it do, it will need something more.' My
thanks are, therefore, due to Benedict Tutty of my own community for offering to me his drawings on the theme of light: the
light which shines, transforms, gives guidance, even when an
effort must be made and which will, sometimes, seem to be completely insufficient while reminding us that it is always somewhere there.

But let me come back to that document which I have mentioned
and which has inspired so many in the past. It is the famous Rule
of Benedict and it must always be the basis of authentic
Benedictine life. Throughout the chapters of this book, I have referred to it quite frequently and have, moreover, quoted what
appears to me to be its most important parts. But I include as
well some sections from those ancient legends which were edited
so long ago by Pope St Gregory the Great. They may not be a
'Life of Benedict' according to historical expectations of today
but they communicate an insight into who he was which has, in
its own way and down the ages, helped to mould what could be
called 'the Benedictine mind'. The authors of that 'Life', and of
the Rule itself, have certainly assisted in the moulding of my
own, and both of them, as glancing at the 'notes' will show, have
been the principal and pivotal inspirers of my effort here.

But there are also many others who have influenced the writing
of this book. Among them, in the first place, are those people
(mostly monks) who, by their words and by their lives, have
helped me to appreciate the value of the Benedictine Way and
some of them are mentioned or referred to in my text. However,
there are also those who have encouraged me, in different ways,
to persevere in what I started out to do and who, by their suggestions, and at times objections, have not only steered my
thoughts but, in so doing, have been instrumental in what has
been written, too. To them, and to all those who have corrected

what appeared at times to be innumerable typing errors, I am deeply grateful.

It is for the readers, now, to take the process further! If the Benedictine Way as I present it is attractive, may they find that it, in many ways, can be a sure and fruitful guide. If they accept the wisdom of those sections of the Rule which have been quoted, may it lead them, as it has led many in the past, to find God's presence in the people whom they meet each day and in the world around. Above all, as they journey on, may they discover in themselves that peace, that *Pax*, which has become, not just a motto for the Benedictine Way, but the promise-bearing title of this present book, as well.

Part One

Benedict himself

I never went to Nursia!

Although I lived in Rome for three years as a student and, from there, went out to see important Benedictine places I neglected visiting that little mountain town where Benedict himself, according to St Gregory,[1] was born. No doubt a number of my fellow Benedictine students undertook that pilgrimage but, I, apparently, did not consider it worthwhile. And, looking back, that, now, seems rather strange.

Since those now distant days I have, of course, read quite a lot about St Benedict and yet I must admit that I have never found an author who convinced me that, in my ignoring Nursia, I had made some unfortunate mistake. I have not, for example, found a scholar who suggested that without at least a visit to that place where he had spent his first and formative years I would not ever understand St Benedict himself. Perhaps, of course, the day will come when I will make that pilgrimage and find that I must then apologize to Nursia for my neglect! But, at this moment, all that I can do is just to echo what that little mountain town appears to say. It is: 'I am myself not necessary for your search. St Benedict, whom you desire to understand, is now a person who reflects a wider and a greater world.' And that, indeed, is true. He has, as we I hope will see, a wisdom which belongs, not only to his place of birth, or even to his native land, but to the whole of Europe and, indeed, to other continents as well – and to all ages too!

But let us go back to the first few centuries which followed his. It was a period when groups of people, both in Italy and further north, discovered that the words which he had written in his Rule were wise and useful for the living of their daily lives. And so, in what have now become the lands of different European states, a network of new monasteries began to form themselves according to that Rule which they had somehow found. And then, of course, through those same monasteries the influence of Benedict began to spread and mould, in different ways, the lives of other people, too.

This radiation of the Benedictine spirit was achieved, not only through the ordinary contact which the monks, or nuns, would have established with the people of the area in which they lived, but also through the sermons which would have been preached to those who came to worship in their monastery church. Moreover, it would frequently have been achieved through civil legislation too, for abbots in the Middle Ages often had a voice in parliament, as well. Indeed, according to historians, the wisdom of St Benedict became, through all these avenues, one of the most important elements in building up the unity of Europe in those often-troubled times.[2]

In our present century that contribution of St Benedict to secular society has been acknowledged in a special and a hope-filled way. In 1947, for example, when the devastating war was over and so many Europeans had to turn around and start to build their lives anew, Pope Pius XII looked back to what St Benedict had done and spoke of him as a 'Father' of the continent.[3] In 1964, Pope Paul VI, when consecrating the rebuilt basilica of Monte Cassino, added his appreciation of what Benedict had done. But, since the movement towards the unity of Europe had, by then, begun that Pope, who hoped that it would be attained, decided to proclaim St Benedict to be, not just a father but 'the principal patron of all Europe'[4] for that time. More recently, in 1980, (which was celebrated as the 1500th anniversary of Benedict's own birth) the present Pope, John Paul ll, called to mind this declaration of his predecessor and expressed his own particular wish: that we today, inspired by Benedict, would find again 'the meaning of existence.'[5] That, indeed, would be a treasure well worthwhile!

However, all these phrases come from churchmen and could, therefore, be dismissed as merely pious wishes. Consequently, it would be most interesting if some of those who are involved in legislating for our new community of Europe were to say the same. It is, perhaps, not likely that they will. And yet, according to one Benedictine abbot, some at least have recognised the influence of Benedict in ages past. Moreover, they have even, although unofficially, expressed their personal desire that that same Spirit which once animated him would flow into this present age as well.

Such statements and expressions of appreciation are, however, still too limited for one whose feast is celebrated, not just in the continent of Europe, but throughout the world. His influence in recent centuries has spread to all the other continents and monasteries of Benedictine monks and nuns are found in them today. His wisdom has been welcomed and, not just in areas which have a lot of European roots, but in the very different worlds of India and sub-Saharan Africa. We have good reason, therefore, to declare that Benedict of Nursia appears to be one of those universal figures who have much to give to people everywhere. Perhaps we can say, too, that he is one who can belong to everyone!

* * *

There are some valuable details in the life of Benedict which we ought to consider here and one of them is certainly that, at a certain stage, he turned his back on Rome and all that it was promising at the time! He had, according to St Gregory, been sent there by his family to study and, no doubt, to qualify for some respectable career. But, when he saw the way his fellow-students lived and realised that life in that imperial city could become an obstacle to what, for him, was even more important than a good position in this world, he knew the time had come for making his own personal decision about what he had to do. And so, according to St Gregory, 'he drew back the foot which he had placed on the threshold of the world'.[6] He left his studies and he cut connections with his family (which may suggest that they were less than sympathetic to his plans), and set out for the hills to lead a more explicitly religious kind of life.

The message which St Gregory desired his readers to receive is fairly clear. It is that they, as well, should seek God in their lives and be prepared to turn their backs on anything which would impede them in their search. That would at times, he knew, be difficult. Of course, not many would discover that they were being called to go into the hills to live a hermit's life; that would be only for the few. But all who hear his call can find that God is asking them to make decisions which are just as radical in their own lives as was the one of Benedict in his!

In this connection there are two expressions which could be considered here. The first is from the Rule itself; the second from the Life which Pope St Gregory composed. They are, however, complementary to each other, one proclaiming what we should not do, the other what we should.

The first expression is a simple admonition though, of course, it can be unexpectedly demanding, too. It is, to quote McCann's translation of the Rule: 'to avoid worldly conduct'[7] or, to keep the flavour of the Latin text, 'to make oneself a stranger to the manners of the world'. It is what Benedict himself was doing when he set out for the hills. It is what others do in different ways as their own lives unfold. The meaning which it has for each of us, however, we must ponder for ourselves.

The second phrase is one of Pope St Gregory himself. He tells us that St Benedict left everything in order 'to please God alone.'[8] To please! That phrase suggests, not only that St Benedict was 'seeking God', but also that he was prepared to do what God seemed to be asking every day. In his case, that would have involved 'avoiding earthly conduct' or whatever would entangle him in contradictory things. It is not too surprising, therefore, that St Benedict would speak of his devotion as the service of a soldier to a powerful king![9]

These two expressions, we could note, sum up for us that 'turning from' and 'turning to' which are the essence of that most important Benedictine virtue of conversion which we will be able to consider in more detail later on.

* * *

Benedict, when he made his way into the hills arrived, eventually, at a place called Subiaco, which is fifty miles or so from Rome. And there he met, or was discovered by a person who, already, had been living as a monk. Romanus was his name. They spoke together and when he, Romanus, realised what Benedict desired he 'helped him, providing him with a monk's habit and ministering to his wants as he was able'.[10] Thus, with the assistance of a seasoned monk, the youthful Benedict began his own monastic life. And for a dwelling-place he chose a cave up on the mountainside!

This is intriguing but it is, as well, a little strange because the Rule itself implies that hermiting is something which should not be chosen, if at all, until the candidate has lived for quite a while in some community. In chapter one we read of Anchorites and Hermits and it says that they are:

> those who not in the first fervour of their conversion, but after long probation in a monastery, having learnt in association with many brethren how to fight against the devil, go out well-armed from the ranks of the community to the solitary combat of the desert.[11]

There is, of course, a lot of wisdom in deferring such a difficult and hazardous existence until one is more mature and, maybe, it was from his own experience that Benedict decided that, in fact, that was the better course. However, since we have no evidence to make us think that he may have regretted making the decision which he made, he may be just accepting here the teaching of the writers who preceded him. It was that, normally at least, one should not start a hermits' life until one has been helped by 'many brethren' to cope with all the ordinary things which can attack and worry us each day.

And yet! And yet a period of solitude from time to time can be of value to us all. I can recall a recent Abbot Primate saying that he felt like recommending such a hermiting experience to everyone and, if I am not mixing up his statement with that of another, he referred to Subiaco as a place which would, for reasons which are obvious, be very suitable for monks. Not everybody, however, will be able to climb up the mountain to that 'sacro speco' (which was Benedict's own 'sacred cave') but everyone can surely find some comparable spot which is much nearer home. It does not really matter where it is so long as it allows us to withdraw from all the pressures of our ordinary lives and, when we have reviewed them calmly, to be still and to enjoy the Presence which is liberating us. The Subiaco chapter in the life of Benedict reminds us of this need and of the God who in the silence can transform us as he did St Benedict himself.

* * *

For three whole years St Benedict continued living in his hermitage and then, St Gregory informs us, he was found by local shepherds who were pasturing their sheep. Perhaps they found him just by accident. Perhaps they spied him from afar and then, deciding to investigate, climbed up the mountainside. In any case, when they discovered him, they found a person who impressed them greatly for St Gregory was able to declare that:

> coming to know the servant of God, they were converted...
> to a Christian life.[12]

And then those shepherds, we are told, went home and spoke to others in their area about the strange but fascinating person whom they met. And so a lot of other people climbed the mountain and, when they discovered for themselves the man of God, they too were equally impressed. They kept returning, we are told, and, while they frequently brought him some food to eat, what they received was more important still. It was, to quote St Gregory, a 'nourishment for life'.[13]

We touch a very strange and yet important mystery here. It is that he, who did not seek to influence the lives of others, for he chose to be a hermit in the hills, became the unexpected instrument of God. That paradox appears again throughout the so-called Benedictine centuries which followed in the Church. The monks and nuns who lived in medieval monasteries did not intend to be such influential people in the building up of Europe but God used them all the same. We will speak more of that. But, for the moment, let us simply note that God quite frequently gives us his most important gifts through people who do not set out to influence our lives and that he also uses us, at times, to

touch the lives of other people when we are not really trying to
do very much for them at all!

* * *

Some of those who listened to the word of Benedict must have
expressed a wish to stay for we are told that soon a small community began to grow. Indeed, it would appear that as his fame
began to spread a lot of others also came and even stayed for we
are told that there were, not just one, but twelve communities established in the area of Subiaco. Pope St Gregory describes it
thus:

> (Benedict) was able with the all-powerful help of our Lord
> Jesus Christ to build twelve monasteries there, in each of
> which he set an abbot and twelve monks.[14]

And so St Benedict became the founder, not just of a monastery,
but of a whole monastic settlement! It was, within the war-torn
and disintegrating world around him, an oasis of tranquillity
and peace and one which must have been a powerful and
prophetic sign to many of what their society in many ways
could be.

However, he was not to stay at Subiaco very long. A situation
which was very difficult arose and Benedict decided that he
should move to another place. And so, with some disciples, he
set out and travelled south until he came to Monte Cassino
where he stopped and where he built another monastery which
has, like Subiaco, been associated with him to this present day.

This new establishment upon Cassino has, since then, been frequently rebuilt for it was frequently destroyed. The present
buildings on that mountain, therefore, are a witness, not just to
St Benedict himself nor to the place where he was finally in-
terred, but to the indestructability of that desire for God which
was personified in him and which can often bubble up in our
own lives as well. It was, moreover, to facilitate the growth of
that desire that, while he lived there with his own community,
he wrote the famous Rule which we can now consider in some
detail here.

The Rule

St Benedict was not the founder of an order. He was one who wrote a book,[1] a book which had, as we have seen, a lot of influence upon the lives of many people down the ages and in many countries, too. To use a metaphor, St Benedict was not the planter of a tree which grew and grew and put forth branches far and wide until it covered almost all the earth. He simply nurtured one small plant and watched it blossom where it was. But, then, when he had gone, the seeds of that small plant were blown to other places where they settled and, quite frequently, took root. That plant was the community which lived on Monte Cassino and the seeds were copies of the Rule which he composed while living with his first disciples there. The monasteries which came to birth in other places, therefore, were not parts of some great centralised concern but members of a family which was as varied as the members of a family can be. What made them one, and what still keeps them all together, is the wisdom and the vision which they have discovered through their study and their living of the Rule.

It is this Rule which I am hoping in these pages to explore. It is itself, of course, a 'Rule for Monks' and so, inevitably, much of what it says will not apply to people who do not live cloistered and monastic lives. But, on the other hand, the Rule of Benedict, reveals an understanding of that human nature which we all possess and of that art of true relating both to one another and to God which is of interest to us all. It is on this, its deeper, level that it speaks to everyone. A recent writer wrote:

> Because there are no differences in the fundamental experiences of Christian faith between those of monks...and those of other Christians ... the Rule of Benedict (can) offer an inspiration for Christianity at large.[2]

And I believe that what he wrote is right.

One of the reasons why this Benedictine Rule can be of universal value is because it echoes so much of a rich tradition which had been developing before it was composed. St Benedict, in other words, did not sit down and write a document out of his own experience alone. He knew and had reflected on the writings of so many authors who preceded him and, having a respect for what they said, he let their words flow through his mind and influence his own. He knew, for instance, what is now referred to as the Rule of the Master and, indeed, he used large sections of what that anonymous author wrote.[3] He also knew the works of people like Augustine, Basil and John Cassian and accepted much of what they taught.[4] He knew, of course, and quoted frequently, the Scriptures which, for monks as well as for all Christians was considered as the fundamental and essential rule. From all these sources, therefore, he composed for his community at Monte Cassino and, indeed, for others which might want to use it, too, the document which since then bears his name. Most probably a copy of it was dispatched to the foundation which he made at Terracina[5] but a recent writer, Ester de Waal, believes that Benedict's particular reflection of a great tradition can enrich each reader in this present age as well:

> I believe that the Rule is able to feed the divergent streams within each of us because it is itself made up of divergent streams.[6]

And so, in this book, let us try to isolate and to admire some of the most important of those streams and trust that, as we do, they will lead us, as they have led so many in the past, towards that promised ocean of fulfilment and of satisfying life.

This Rule, which has had such an influence, is read aloud in every Benedictine monastery and not just once but three times every year. Indeed editions of the Rule which we can buy quite often print, beside each paragraph, the dates on which that section should be read. But 'where' and 'when' that reading will take place will not be everywhere the same. All I can say for certain is that in my monastery the predetermined passage can be heard before the Night Prayer of the day and, therefore, in the open-to-the-public church. This does not mean that every visitor or guest will be so fascinated that, a little later, in the parlour, he or she will start some interesting discussion on the section which was read! Yet, sometimes, some will make some comment and, occasionally, some will take the matter further and reflect upon the value of its content for today.

The sections of the Rule which tend to stimulate a quick response are, naturally, those, which sound a bit unusual, and even humorous, today. Some guests will, therefore, for example, joke and say that it is strange that monks are told to take off, not their clothing, but 'their knives' before they go to bed!

> Let them sleep clothed ... but not with their belts, so that they
> may not have their knives at their sides when they are sleeping, and be cut by them in their sleep.[7]

Presumably, however, this was good advice when Benedict was writing down his Rule and, maybe, it was even the result of some unfortunate experience, as well! But, then, another guest, and on another day, may comment on another line and say: 'Is it not also strange that, while the Rule allows the sick to take a bath as often as they need, it seems to legislate against the hygiene of the others?'

> To the healthy, and especially to the young let them be granted
> seldom.[8]

That, certainly, is not what people would expect to hear today! But, then, let us go back again to when St Benedict was writing for, in his time and, indeed, until quite recently, to take a bath would have implied much more than just the simple turning of a tap! Moreover, it would hardly have involved the comfort or the privacy which we can now, so easily, presume.

But there are other sayings in the Rule which can impress the listener in the church although no comment may, in fact, be made on them at all. They may be simply noted and accepted and allowed to work below one's consciousness while life itself goes on! And yet, I do seem to remember someone saying that St Benedict appears to have been very wise and understanding and, as far as I can now recall, that was because he recognised the very simple fact that some of those for whom he wrote might have some special dietary need! Indeed, in legislating for the food which monks should eat, he said that there should be on every table:

> two cooked dishes ... so that he who perchance cannot eat of
> the one, may make his meal of the other.[9]

That was, certainly, considerate but there are many other places
in the Rule which manifest the same humane concern, not least
the one which tells the abbot, who had very great responsibili-
ties, that he should learn how to adapt himself to many dispositions and accommodate himself to all.[10]

The abbot was to be considerate[11] in everything he had to do but
so, too, was the Cellarer, that key official of the monastery who
was in charge of the material provisions of the place. He would
have been, of course, by his position one to whom the others
would have come for many different things and sometimes he,
no doubt, was tired while there were other times when he might
not have had in stock what one of them so urgently required! It
was with situations such as these in mind, and conscious of the
way that one can easily react, that, in the chapter on the Cellarer,
St Benedict decreed:

> above all things let him have humility and, if he has nothing
> else to give, let him give a good word in answer; for it is writ-
> ten: 'A good word is above the best gift'.[12]

This is a good word in itself and, since it is not in his major
source, (i.e. The Rule of the Master) it may be a contribution of St
Benedict himself. It, certainly, reveals an author who combines a
deep respect for others with a sensitivity to their essential needs.
It is, however, most unlikely that what he once recommended to
the Cellarer of his own monastery is not what he would recommend to everyone who has to deal with other people and their
needs, wherever they may be!

To enter more into the spirit of this rightly-famous Rule the best
approach would be, without a doubt, to visit some community
of Benedictines and to spend a little time with them. Of course,
one can just go down to a local bookshop and obtain a copy of
the Rule to read and study by oneself. But, even if one does do
that (and it is not a bad idea) there is an added value in the actual
experience which such a visit could provide. It often is the lived-
out understanding of the Rule which can explain it best.
However, since not every reader will be able to make such a
visit, I am going to include in many of my chapters a description

of those aspects of the life which, normally, a guest would see. This will, I hope, provide some kind of literary substitute but I would also like it to be taken as an exercise of that essential hospitality which was so recommended by St Benedict himself.

And so, I hope that what I write will stir good memories in those who have, in fact, been welcomed at some monastery and, at the same time, be a kind of introduction for the rest. For everyone who reads this book, however, what I hope is that it will provide a better and a deeper understanding of what we might call 'The Benedictine Way for All'.

Part Two

A Balanced Way of Life

The visitor who spends a few days at a Benedictine monastery becomes aware, to some extent at least, of different things which happen there. Initially the guest will notice that the whole community assembles in the church some four or five or even seven times a day for periods of prayer.[1] Then he or she may come to realise that in between those periods a lot of work is also done and, often, what that work may actually be. For some of the community it may be teaching in a school. For others it may be the cultivation of the land. For others still it may be making works of art in metal or in wood and some will, certainly, be occupied in day-to-day administration of some kind. Each monastery according to the talents of its members and the needs of the locality, may be a little different from the next but each will have its own collection of accumulated works.

A guest, however, who has thought about this alternating rhythm between work and prayer may say in conversation that the Benedictine life appears to be a very balanced one, indeed! And that, in fact, is what the author of the Rule intended it to be. However, such a comment by a guest may often be much more an indication of the speaker's life than of the life which he or she has really only just begun to glimpse! It may, in other words, reveal a certain lack of balance in that person's life which, in the context of the monastery, has been perceived more clearly than it was before and which, to some extent, is now regretted, too! If that is so, we can, perhaps, conclude that the initial consequence of contact with the Benedictine way has been a new capacity to recognise how necessary such a balance really is.

At times this new awareness will occasion a discussion in the Guest House on what one should do! Suggestions may, of course, be made but, when the basic problem for some individual is that there is no work at all for him or her to do, there is not anything to balance and quite often for the moment not too much to say. Such situations can be sad and soul-destroying for the victim, too (as anyone who has been unemployed will know). The question which emerges here, however, is 'how would St Benedict himself react to such a crisis?' and there must have been a lot of them in his own troubled times. The answer is not given clearly but, as often happens with this kind of problem, there are clues.

We could begin by saying that St Benedict declared that: 'idleness is the enemy of the soul', [2] but that is not immediately helpful for he spoke within the context of a small society which he had organised himself and which successfully provided work for everyone and often satisfying work as well. Today, our lives are in a bigger and a much more complicated world and there is little we can do to organise it in the way that we would like. We can but play our part! Our part! Perhaps, that is precisely what St Benedict would have us do. Perhaps, what he would say to us who do have work is that it would be good, not just to be aware of the employment crisis (which we surely are), but to facilitate in own our neighbourhood the building of a new society in which there could be opportunities for other people to use their own talents, too. Facilitate! What that implies for each of us we have, of course, to ponder for ourselves. But, then, if some of those who have no work discover some and then discover, too, that they have energy and interest to become involved in other things as well, it may be time to think aloud with them about that regulating quality, that balance which can also give a new potential to their lives. And so we play our part! If the disciples of St Benedict in ages past were able to contribute to the building up of Europe, why can his disciples of today not, somehow, for at least a few of those around them do the same?

However, what St Benedict would, certainly, desire is that all those who have a basic work-insertion in society should learn how best to spend their other hours in useful rather than, perhaps, in idle ways. He would, moreover, urge them, then, to punctuate all that they do each day with periods of prayer. Or, if

you would prefer, he would like us to learn how to be open to
the One who works through what we do, so that, through us, the
world may really grow into a better place and, in its own way,
give its Maker praise!

* * *

Sometimes a guest may quote in this connection: 'Ora et Labora'
(pray and work), a motto which is printed on the walls of many
monasteries today. It is a motto which refers to those two elements of Benedictine life which we have noted and it is a motto
which the writers of the nineteenth century liked to use.[3] But
here, perhaps, it should be pointed out that 'Ora et labora' does
not mean (as it is sometimes said) that 'prayer *is* work' or, on the
other hand, that 'work *is* prayer'. There may, of course, be truth
in both of those assertions and, indeed, there surely is. But what
the famous nineteenth century motto indicates is simply two activities which, while connected, are distinct and separate in
themselves.

But let us here personify these two activities and, for that purpose, use those well-known women of the Gospel story, Martha
and her sister, Mary. This, in fact, is what a number of those
nineteenth century Benedictine writers have already done. For
them the sister who was busy doing many things became a symbol of the element of work while Mary, sitting at the feet of Jesus
and absorbing all he said, became a symbol of the element of
prayer. This is, indeed, most interesting because for centuries
those sisters had been taken as the representatives of either the
contemplative or active orders in the Church. Thus Mary repre-
sented Carmelites, Poor Clares and others who observed a strict
enclosure while the busy Martha was adopted by the active or,
as we might say today, the apostolic congregations in the
Church. The Benedictine writers of the nineteenth century, however, knew that those two elements need to be nurtured in us all.
Each one of us, no matter who we are, is both a Martha who can
serve a neighbour and a Mary who, too frequently perhaps, does
not find all the space and freedom she requires![4]

Both prayer and work together give a balance to our lives and in this balance we are able, say so many, to be free. Thus, these two elements have been described by a poetic Maurus Wolter as 'two wings which lift us to the heights'.[5]

However, we can add to our poetic flight by saying that 'two wings' depend upon the wind to lift and carry them if they are to attain 'the heights'. Moreover, since the 'wind' is 'air', is 'breath of God', is 'Spirit', what we need in both our prayer and work is, therefore, God's own Spirit blowing through our lives. It is the unifying and the liberating force.

* * *

The Rule refers to these two elements but, if it does, it speaks of them, as we shall see, not only with a sharper focus, but within a somewhat wider framework, too.

Concerning prayer, one must begin by saying that the Rule says less about the *how* of prayer, especially in private, than it does of *what* we ought to say when we have all assembled in the church. However, it presents this latter as a most important exercise and one which it is ready to describe as *Opus Dei*, which means 'Work of God'. This title, it should here be noted, has not anything at all to do with that society which started only recently in Spain. The *Opus Dei*, for St Benedict and for the people of his time, is prayer and praise and it is offered up, like incense, to the One who calls us to himself.

To call this rather wonderful activity a 'work', however, does require an explanation, and especially because I have, till now, kept prayer and work apart. And yet, as I have also intimated, prayer at times can be laborious, as well! Indeed when it implies participating with a lot of other people, not just once or twice, but every day and for a life-time, too, an effort which is almost super-human is required. However, in the last analysis, the 'work' in prayer is done, as *Opus Dei* may suggest, much more by God than by ourselves for it is he who, in his Spirit, works through us as we approach him through our prayer. Thus, it is he who, through us, gives himself the praise and glory which we have the privilege of offering, as well. It, therefore, is not too surprising to discover that the author of the Rule can use one of his absolutes and say, 'let nothing be put before the Work of God'.[6]

It is, he seems to say, important for us to be part of this dynamic movement which is no less than the life of the divinity itself!

But, for the moment, let us note that in another chapter of the Rule the author speaks about, not only 'work' (the second element of Benedictine life) but also about 'reading' of a certain kind. He says:

> The brethren, therefore, should be occupied at stated hours
> in manual labour and again at other times in sacred reading,[7]

So there is, in fact, an extra element which begs for some consideration, too!

As for the 'work' (we'll take that first), St Benedict does not give us a list of things which we should do nor does he tell us what the ordinary members of his own communities did every day. However, in a later chapter of the Rule, he mentions that:

> the monastery ... should be so arranged that all necessary
> things, such as water, mill, garden, and various crafts may be
> within the enclosure.[8]

That does seems to suggest that there was a supply of necessary work which would not only have been done, but, probably, each day as well. In later centuries a lot of monks became involved in work which was more intellectual than manual and, while that offered no small contribution to the Church and to the world, it did upset a certain balance in the life of those concerned. However, what may be of interest to us here is that not only do some monks today desire the simpler life-style of the past, but many ordinary folk are introducing into theirs some kind of manual dimension, too. They seem to feel that it, not only makes them one with the environment in which they live, but that it adds, in some way, to the quality of their own human lives as well.

Finally, concerning that new element, the 'sacred reading' of St Benedict, there is a lot which should be said, and will, but, here, let me just speak about the term itself. The 'sacred reading' in the Rule is 'lectio', or sometimes 'lectio divina' for the reading often was the Word of God or some book which explained it in some satisfying way. This 'lectio divina' for St Benedict's disciples occupied, it seems, a kind of a middle ground between those periods in which some manual activity was done (and during which the mind was free to ponder what was read!) and those which were reserved for formal prayer (in which the Scriptures occupied a quite considerable part). Today, however, while a lot of people read a lot, their reading, even of the Scriptures, can quite often be no more than just a mental exercise and so much less than what the Lectio Divina of St Benedict implied. We, therefore, need to rediscover something of that ancient art. We need to read the Word of God in such a way that it will have an opportunity to seep into our hearts and there begin to influence, not just our prayer, but every aspect of our lives as well.

And so there are, not two, but three parts to the Benedictine day. Or, putting that another way, we could say that the Rule provides for some activity which will involve the body and for some activity which will involve the mind and, finally, for opportunities in which the spirit which is in us can expand. These three are separate and each has to be catered for and yet each one of them depends to some extent upon the other two. The one which holds a very special key, however, is the one which cultivates the mind. If it, that is the mind, is furnished with the right ideas the body will, without a doubt, be healthier than it would be with other ones and, on the other hand, the spirit which is in us will be able to be free. That spirit is, of course, not just our own but, mingling with it all the time, that other greater Spirit which can soar and which itself is infinite and no less than divine!

* * *

As we juggle these three elements of life – our work, our lectio, our prayer – we will begin to notice that, although we need, indeed, to juggle them, they are not all identical as are the objects which the juggler in a circus juggles with such ease. Thus, we will start to notice that our lectio and prayer evoke much deeper levels of ourselves than work will often do and that our prayer at times, is able to awake in us the deepest part of all. Indeed, it touches, sometimes, and releases the essential centre of our being and when that occurs we will not feel the need for many words or even many thoughts. We will be happy and content just to be there! That is a precious moment and a vitalising one which, then, will energise us to return to lectio with new enthusiasm and to face again, with confidence, the challenges of work. These three components have, indeed, a kind of hierarchy of their own and yet they do have one important thing in common with the objects which the circus-juggler has: if one is not caught properly the others will, most probably, begin to fall!

But, as we play with parables, let us admire an image which that writer on the Rule, Esther de Waal, enjoys. It is the way the ribbing on the ceiling of a medieval building rises and converges at the high-up central boss.

> Stand beneath that triumph of later Gothic building and you find pillar and arch, rib and vault are brought together in one great harmonious unity.[9]

And so, as you will see, it does. But focus on that unifying boss! It symbolises our own calm and prayerful moments which, as we are able to discover, can not only hold together all the many and distracting bits and pieces which make up our every day, but quietly support them, too. Or, if you would prefer, think of the hub which is the centre of an ordinary wheel! It is the still point in a moving world! But it allows the spokes of energy to emanate and hold the rim which, in succeeding places, makes its contact with the passing ground! That, too, portrays the moment and the influence of prayer!

* * *

The monk, for whom St Benedict was writing, would have had the help of his community to keep alive these three essential elements. Indeed his life was structured for him in a way which guaranteed them an allotted time each day. In this more hectic age, however, life in monasteries is seldom so determined. So, because of all the many things which can absorb the time and energies of Benedictine monks and nuns, they often have to make an effort of their own if they desire to have some manual activity and, even, if they wish to integrate into their lives a period of lectio each day. The same, of course, is true for all those non-monastic Benedictines in the world. But they have one more problem to resolve: they may not even have a prayer-time guaranteed!

This leads us to a thought which is, no doubt, for most of us today a vital and important one. It is that, if we are to grow as Christians, we require encouragement and some kind of support. We need, in other words, to be a part of some kind of community, be it an ordinary parish one or some particular grouping of like-minded and committed friends. But we need, too, perhaps within that very group, a few with whom, from time to time, we can sit down and share such thoughts as those which come to us in lectio and who, through sharing theirs, can motivate us to go back to our own lectio and, there, discover more! We need, especially however, all those people who can help us in an unbelieving age to be aware of 'things which are not seen'[10] and to accept a God of love into the many ups and downs which seem to form the pattern of many human lives.

* * *

Let me close this chapter with the comment of a most perceptive guest. We had been talking for a while about how difficult it often is to persevere in keeping all of these three elements alive. For some short periods we seem to get them right but, then, another crisis comes and, even though we are surrounded by supportive friends, we lose control and life seems to collapse. 'What is important', she declared, 'is, not that we will never fail, but that we keep on trying'. She was right! What matters in the long run is, not that we always manage to achieve our perfect plan, but that, when it is not attained, we have the patience to relax and then, when we are ready, to begin to work at it again. However, some day all those 'downs', those 'unsuccessful moments' may appear in retrospect to have been part of God's much greater plan. We will discover that, if not within each single day, within the gradual unfolding of our lives an unexpected balancing of all these elements was, in a strange way, operating there.

Lectio Divina

In the Guest-house, and quite frequently in every room, there will be found some books which those who come to stay awhile may read. This seems to be a useful service for there can be periods when guests will find themselves alone and when a 'literary friend' can often be a help. But, in the very act of reading what some recommended author has to say, not only can the reader get some profitable thoughts, but he or she is able to become, in some way, bonded to all those who have already read that book and have assimilated what it says! To follow that particular line of thought, we can maintain that, through such reading, guests are brought a little more into the inner life of the community which welcomes them for, in the Rule, such reading is encouraged and much time is designated for it, too.

* * *

The Rule provides for two or three hours 'lectio' each day. In chapter 48 we read:

> From Easter until September the 14th, the brethren shall start work in the morning and … from the fourth hour till the sixth let them apply themselves to reading.

And, a little further down, when that same chapter is referring to the other seasons of the year, we find these exhortations:

> from September 14th. to the beginningof Lent let them apply themselves to reading up to the end of the second hour,

and:

> in the days of Lent let them apply themselves to their reading from the morning until the end of the third hour.

Those 'hours', of course, were those of Roman times and so not similar to those we have today. They were not counted from one midnight to the next but through the separated periods of darkness and of light, which varied in their length according to the time of year and which were, then, divided into twelve. However, what concerns us here is not the Roman way of calculating time, but the importance which this period of lectio had for the author of the Rule. Indeed, compared to some monastic writers who preceded him, St Benedict appears to have provided for this 'lectio', not just a lot of time each day, but what could be considered 'prime time', too![1] There must be something we can learn from that!

* * *

The book, however, which should always be available for guests is that one which we call the Bible, or 'the book' (for that is what the Greek word really means).[2] For people like St Benedict it was essential reading though his comment in the final chapter of the Rule does little more than hint at the intrinsic value which it has. 'What page or utterance of the Old and New Testaments is not a most unerring rule of human life?' he simply and provocatively asks.[3] And yet he does refer in that same chapter to some other books as well. They are, presumably, the ones which he considered to be helpful for the monks of his own time as they were persevering in their own monastic lives. But, since the life they lived was ultimately built upon the Word of God, such recommended authors would have led their readers back to Scripture which was always understood to be the fundamental and essential Christian guide.

Today, however, if there is a problem for a would-be reader it is often, not about the way to read the Scriptures but, with all the books which are available, which one of them to choose! Indeed I can remember asking one old monk if it was really necessary to read all the many books which he was recommending at the time. His answer I remember too and, as it may be useful to some readers, I will quote him here. 'Read', he said, 'as widely as you can, but keep returning to that book which is the measure of them all'. There was no doubt, at all, about which book he had in mind!

Perhaps this is the place to say that, if the Bible is 'the book of

books' and if it is (as we believe) inspired, to speak of 'lectio divina' is extremely apt for, through its pages, it is God himself who
speaks. The fathers of the second Vatican Council knew that,
too, and so in one of their decrees they solemnly declared:

> In the sacred books the Father who is in heaven comes lov-
> ingly to meet his children and talks with them.[4]

Thus when we speak today of reading Scripture as a 'sacred
reading' we should note that what is sacred is, not just *our reading* of the word, but the *very word itself*.[5] Indeed the liturgy is able
to remind us of this fact! When, for example, we observe the
book being carried in, with some solemnity, in the procession to
the altar (as it sometimes is) and when we see the Gospel being
incensed by the deacon just before it is proclaimed, we have a
visual reminder of the sacred power which is being honoured
there. Perhaps, in our own day and age when books are plentiful
and can be tossed about so easily, it might be good to treat our
Bibles with a little extra care! In any case, it is important to approach them with a certain reverence if we are to receive from
them the loving and transforming message which they offer to
us all.

* * *

And yet to treat the Bible in a special way is really not enough.
The word needs to be read but also to be heard! That happens in
the liturgy, of course, for there the text is read aloud for everyone to hear but, when St Benedict was writing, it could have occurred as well when somebody was sitting in a corner with some
volume for himself. According to a recognised authority, in such
a situation:

> the reader usually pronounced the words with his lips, at
> least in a low tone, and, consequently, he hears the sentence
> seen by the eyes.[6]

That was, no doubt, a slower way of getting through a book than
methods which we use today but it appears to have been no less
an effective one and, probably, in ways more satisfying, too.

In order, therefore, to appreciate this method just a little more let
us imagine, for a moment, that a time-machine has brought us
back into the eighth, or seventh, century and that we now are

walking in a medieval cloister while the monks are reading there. We see, in different places different monks, each with a scroll or book but – here is the important point – we actually hear them, too! A low but constant murmuring, (to use a word which often has another meaning in the Rule![7]), pervades the area. St Benedict referred to this as 'meditatio', which did not mean for him the silent mental pondering, which 'meditation' often means today, but, simply, the pronouncing of each word in such a way that it was able to be heard as well as to be seen. And so, not only could the words which were being read by all those ancient monks soak into them through their own eyes but through their ears as well. Indeed, they even entered through the very movements of their mouths! The actual articulation of each syllable would have allowed the reader to experience what we might call the contours, or the 'feel', of every word.

But let us walk a little more around this medieval cloister and become aware that some of those who read do not read on and on but tend, at times, to stop and to repeat some word or verse or phrase. It is as if they want to try to penetrate its meaning more and more. It is as if they want to actually taste the message which the words contain. Indeed, if we could ask one of those ancient monks why he is reading as he does, it is in that vein that he would quite possibly reply. As a fairly recent writer put it:

> metaphors of tasting and of savouring the words of the Bible come naturally to people who read with their lips and mouths.[8]

And, while some aspects of the Word of God can have, at times, a somewhat bitter taste,[9] the central and abiding message is, the psalmist says, as honey to the mouth![10]

* * *

Let us push another button in our time-machine and come back more or less five hundred years. We will find there a different, and, indeed, a changing, world. We will find people who are reading but a number of them will occasionally stop to *analyse* what they have read and, then, to *draw some intellectual conclusions*. Some will even try to bring together all the information they can glean and make some kind of universal summary.[11] But that, of course, was also good for *knowledge* is important for our lives.

But there were other people who were saying that this new approach to reading did not do sufficient justice to our deepest
human need. What we require, they kept on saying, is not only
knowledge but that *wisdom* which comes through a quiet and
responsive listening to the word. They, therefore, emphasised
for us again the value of 'old-fashioned lectio', although some
also spoke of it in ways that were themselves completely new!
One such was Guigo,[12] a Carthusian monk, who wrote to one of
his Cistercian friends a letter which would later be an inspiration for a lot of other people, too.

There are, says Guigo in this letter, certain stages in our lectio involvement. (Such analysis is certainly a new approach!) He then
explains this statement by proposing for our use the image of a
ladder which is resting on the earth and piercing, at the other
end, the clouds. It is extremely long but Guigo is insisting that
there are not many rungs on it at all. In fact, he says, there are no
more than four. (A method for our progress is about to be proposed!). However, since what he is saying has been helpful to a
lot of people, let us pause and give him our attention, too.

The first rung on the ladder, he declares, is simply that of *reading*. What we choose is not of prime importance here although,
of course, as we begin we will discover certain passages which
are more meaningful than others. For the moment, let us just accept the need to read. Without ascending to that first rung of the
ladder we will never reach the top!

The second rung is called by Guigo *meditation* but, since meditation can have many meanings, *pondering*, perhaps, would be a
better word. In any case the mind is active here and it 'examines
each point thoroughly'.[13] This stage may last a while! Indeed
some people will require more time to ponder what the words
imply than others sometimes will. However, all the time the
mind is pondering it should, says Guigo, keep on searching for
the answer to one very special question. It is 'what is the particular grace which is being offered here and now in this particular
verse?' We may decide that it is, let us say, forgiveness, consolation, patience, joy or something of that kind. But, in the last
analysis, the gift which God is offering is his own Spirit for our

lives! When we, within the context of the thoughts provided by the pondered text, become aware of this the time has, possibly, arrived for us to climb another step.

This third rung is, says Guigo, *prayer*! Perhaps, however, we could change this title, too, for prayer can also mean a lot of different things. To call it *yearning*, therefore, might be better, yearning for that gift of gifts which is being offered to us through the sacred words. This yearning is, however, not just a petition which we formulate, though it can be that too, but something which wells up from deep within ourselves. The mind, it should be noted here, is now at rest. It has completed, for the moment, all that it desires to do and so it is the heart that starts to play the major part. It cries out to the Lord. Perhaps, it had been doing so while all the reading and the pondering was going on but, now, it takes the centre stage and, unencumbered by succeeding thoughts, expresses to the Lord its longing and its need.

But there is still another step! It is a step, or rung, which is important but it probably is one which is quite frequently forgotten, too. It is, however, one on which we can relax for, when we reach it, we are sure that what we had been yearning for is now, to some extent at least, already ours. The Lord, says Guigo, 'does not wait until the longing soul has said its say, but breaks in upon the middle of its prayer'.[14] He calls this step the step of *contemplation*. But, again, it might be useful if we changed his title and referred to it as *calm acceptance* for that is what happens here. We may remain as long as God allows us on this fourth step of the ladder and we should but, if we do 'fall off' and then, perhaps, help others who are, at that moment, 'on the ground', there is no need to be in anyway upset. The ladder will be there when we are ready to begin that climb to quiet contemplation and acceptance once again!

Thus, there are four distinguishable steps on Guigo's ladder and they all can be accomplished with the bible on our knee! Our very *reading* of the word can lead to mental *pondering* and pondering can spark a *yearning* in our hearts and yearning finds its own fulfilment as the gift which God from all eternity desires us to possess is gratefully *accepted* and enjoyed. We will be more equipped to help and serve our neighbour then and, when we do return to reading we, perhaps, will want to focus more and more on those parts which are able to inflame the heart and so dispose us to receive again the gift which God alone can give.

* * *

Let us press another button in our time-machine and travel on until the first part of this very century. There we find an Irish priest who had become a Benedictine monk in Belgium and then abbot of his monastery. He is Columba Marmion[15] and, writing to a nun who had consulted him on prayer, he says:

The principal source of prayer is to be found in holy Scripture read with devotion and reverence and laid up in the heart.[16]

This sentence, which so many people find attractive, echoes the traditional instruction which we have already found but it includes a thought which we have not considered yet. It is that words which have been read with reverence can be engraved upon the heart and, later on, recalled and pondered with advantage once again.

For busy people this can be a very valuable thought. They may have time to read a little Scripture every day but they may also have some opportunities throughout that day (perhaps while waiting for a bus!) to think about what they have read and, maybe, to observe it in a new and fresher light! The words, which have been 'laid up in the heart' can come alive in many different kinds of situations and, not only cause our hearts to yearn for what they seem to offer, but dispose us to receive that promised gift, as well. And so this sentence of Columba Marmion deserves to be inscribed on the initial page of every Bible as it has been, for some decades now, in mine!

* * *

Our last stop in our time-machine, before we reach again the moment which it really is, is (at this time of writing) less than twenty years ago. The person whom we meet there is a Benedictine scholar whom I knew myself. His name is Ambrose Wathen and he says that we should think a little more about the verb 'vacare' which St Benedict quite often used. It means such things as 'to be vacant', 'to be free', 'to be open to' or 'to be empty so that one is able to be filled'. And so, when we read in the Rule: 'let them be open (vacant) to the word',[17] we know that what St Benedict desired was that his readers should allow themselves to be completely filled with that enriching word of God which can transform our lives.

'Vacare' can, however, be an unattractive word for some. It can suggest an aimlessness which those who want to do things do not like. We live in a production-oriented world! Yet even those who are so active can experience a kind of vacancy at certain times. Our Benedictine scholar, Ambrose Wathen, speaks about the way that all of us can sit for hours before a television screen absorbing, without criticism or intent, what it so unrelentingly provides:

> Most people watch T.V. without compulsion for production, without aggression and competition or concern for success. We delight in it, we forget time, we 'vacare' for there is space, time, leisure, freedom for such 'vacatio'.[18]

Perhaps, if we kept on returning to the Scriptures and allowing them to fill our minds, the word of God will worm its way into our lives just as the frequently unbiblically-minded television programmes do. And that could be, not only to our own advantage, but to that of many other people, too!

Prayer

The guest is to be welcomed, says St Benedict, and then invited, in some way, to pray! The Rule, in speaking of these moments, says:

> As soon as a guest is announced let the superior or some brethren meet him with all charitable service. And, first of all, let them pray together.[1]

'First of all', of course, need not be chronological! Each guest has his or her own special needs and 'charitable service' seems to indicate that such needs should be recognised and, therefore, that each person should be welcomed in a way that will allow that person to relax. But since the guest has come to somewhere which has for its *raison d'être* the praise of God, some kind of invitation to participate in that should hardly cause surprise. Indeed, it often may be what is wanted and, perhaps, expected, too.

* * *

The prayer-form which the guest will find when he or she goes into a monastic church is one which is composed of predetermined hymns and reading and a multiplicity of psalms. It may, as such, be very different from the kind of prayer that he or she had been accustomed to till then and yet it does appear to have for many people both a certain fascination and, at times, a very definite appeal. However, when a guest arrives, what he or she may often want to do at first is just to sit and, as it were, absorb the total atmosphere: the sight of many monks, the sound of music and the singing of the psalms, and sometimes, too, the smell of incense which, when used, seems to be wafting everywhere! The booklet which contains the text, and which is often offered, does not seem to be important for them then.

The comment which a guest can make at such a moment can reveal a lot. 'I only want to sit and let it all flow through me,' is quite typical of what is often said. It is the kind of comment which, at times, reminds me of that Scripture verse which says that, when (according to the author) there was nothing but confusion, God's own Spirit came and hovered for a while!

The earth was without form and void (i.e. all confusion) and ... the Spirit of God was moving over the face of the waters.[2] Then, when that had taken place, the Word of God was able to be heard and everything, including as its climax humankind itself, was made.[3] It is the same with every individual. Each one of us can frequently require some time, some quiet, and the hovering of the Spirit if we are to hear that powerful and creative Word. The guest who comes into the church and simply sits may be allowing that same Spirit to begin on him or her its quietly disposing work!

* * *

Sometimes a guest is asked if he or she would like to join the monks in 'choir', that is, in their own section of the church. That may not happen in all monasteries but we reserve some places which those who are staying with us often like to use. In such a situation they can see more clearly what is happening and they certainly can have a better opportunity to follow what is being read or sung. That does not mean that they will feel the need to sing along with what, for all its human imperfections, is a settled choir but somehow in that area they can become aware that they are part of one liturgical community. A subtle presence can be sometimes sensed as quietly involving them!

At times a guest will say that it is strange that all who have assembled there are ordered as they are, that is, in lines which, more or less, are facing one another. What they mean, by such a comment is that they are not all facing in the same direction, as is frequently the case with people in a church, and, probably, that they do not have as a focal point a tabernacle which, for Catholics, is often taken as the norm. However, its exclusion does not signify a disrespect – the Sacrament is probably reserved in some more quiet chapel down the aisle – but that those, who have assembled in the choir, believe that they them-selves are sacramental too! They are themselves the locus where the God, whom they desire to honour, can be found! Those join-ing them are, therefore, being challenged to appreciate that they (both there and, more importantly no doubt, where they reside) are members of a group in which there is a life which if accepted is transformingly divine.

This is, of course, what Jesus had himself already taught. He said to his disciples, 'Where two or three are gathered in my name, there am I in the midst of them,'[4] and so, whenever Christians come together, he is present too! Thus, we are not just 'members of each other'[5] but much more. We are all part of what the Scriptures call the 'Body of the Lord'.[6] It may not be a perfect Body yet, indeed we know that it is not, but, with the help of those same Scriptures which direct our prayer, it can develop and grow strong. Then, as it does, Christ who becomes alive in us will, through us, surely, touch the lives of other people, too.

* * *

The words we hear when we begin to settle down in such a situ-ation can confirm, in different ways, this sense of oneness which we sometimes have. It may be simply by the frequent use of *we* and *us* and *our* instead of *I* and *me* and *mine* as, for example, in that versicle which opens almost every hour:

O God, come to our aid;

O Lord, make haste to help us.[7]

Then, we may notice the collective nouns which we are using in our prayer. There is the *vine*, composed of many branches which we ask the Lord to nurture and protect![8] There is the city, *Zion* or *Jerusalem*, which has so many citizens within its sturdy walls![9] There is, as well, the fairly frequently repeated title *Israel*, which was the name of an ancestral figure in the past but also that of his descendants taken as a whole![10] The word, however, which we will immediately recognise is *sheep*. It may have connota-tions which are over-passive for a lot of people but, in spite of that, it does remind us that we have not only the companionship of many others, but a dedicated shepherd who will lead us all to pastures ever new![11]

The presence of this single figure in the psalms is very strong. If he is not a *shepherd* he may be a *king*[12] or even somebody who does not have a title but is able to personify us all. One thinks, in this connection, of those lamentation psalms in which a solitary singer cries out to the Lord to be delivered from some misery or pain.[13] But one thinks, too, of all those other psalmists who in other psalms express a joy which other people at this very moment also have, and which, moreover, has been promised to us all.[14] Through such *prophetic individuals* we can be drawn towards the centre of that mystery of dying and of rising which has found its ultimate reality in *Christ*. It is his Spirit which is praying in us as our lips and minds are guided by the movement of the psalms.

* * *

The principal preoccupation of the author of the Rule, however, was to guarantee that his disciples would be able to become familiar with the words which they would use when they assembled for their prayer. He, therefore, wrote that those who joined the monastery should live, at first, not with the others who had been there for a while, but 'where the novices work, eat and sleep'.[15] The word which is translated here as 'work', however, really means 'to meditate' and that, as we have seen already, really means 'to read aloud'! In this case what was to be read aloud, and so committed to the memory, was, certainly, those very words which were to have a central and a most important part of their own daily prayer and that, of course, would have included, in a very special way, the psalms.

St Benedict knew that this process of allowing psalms to come alive and, then, to capture all our individual concerns is not one which will be completed during a novitiate, that is within a year, but one which can go on and on as life itself unfolds. So, in another chapter, he declared that:

> those who need a better knowledge of them should devote the times that remains after Matins to the study of the psalms,[16]

and, in another place, aware that everybody and not just a struggling few can always find new meaning and refreshment in those ancient prayers he wrote:

after the meal let them (i.e. the whole community) apply
themselves to reading or to the study of the psalms.[17]
There may, perhaps, be some encouragement for all of us in that!
Indeed, as we go back and read again the psalms and ponder
what they say, we will discover, not just other people who are
sad or glad, but sentiments which all the time are present in ourselves as well. Moreover, as we let those ancient words express
what is most deep in us, they can become more meaningful and
helpful every day.

The purpose of St Benedict, however, was that, when his own
disciples then assembled for their common prayer, both
mind and heart (in them) would be in harmony.[18]
Those words are often quoted but there is no need to understand
them as implying that the mind must always concentrate on
what each word is actually saying as we say or sing the psalms.
That could be quite exhausting and, in fact, restricting too! What
we should do, however, is to ponder them as fully as we can
and, then, in singing them turn our attention to the One to
whom they are addressed. The voice will, then, articulate the
thoughts which will have been digested by the mind but in a
way which will allow the spirit which is in us to flow free!

* * *

Some people say that it is easy to participate in such a prayer as
this when they are at a monastery but that they are not sure how
to continue when they are alone. They sometimes ask, 'what
should we do?' One answer would, of course, be that, because
the content of this type of prayer is taken mostly from the Scriptures, a judicious use of their own Bibles would not be a bad idea
at all. Indeed, a psalm, a section from the Gospels and a time for
private prayer, concluding with the one which Jesus taught us,
would be quite a simple but rewarding formula. But, one could
also say that it would be a good idea to have, as many do, a copy
of the Church's *Daily Prayer*. Although not quite the same as the
monastic prayer, it has the same ingredients and so, in using it,
one can not only have the nourishment which one was given as
a guest but, at the same time, be united in the Spirit with that
welcoming community which, prayerfuly, is reaching out to all!

Commitment

Sometimes a guest may witness a profession in the abbey church. It is a ceremony which not many people ever have a chance to see and so it has a fascination of its own. It is the moment when a novice, who has finished his or her novitiate, commits himself, or herself, to monastic life and, through the living of that life, to God! When it is over some who have been watching it confess that they admire a person who can make such a complete and absolute commitment in this day and age. And others, who may jokingly declare that such a person has decided for 'the better part', are not too sure at all that such a statement is not actually true!

The ceremony which the guest is witnessing, however, happens during Mass. When the readings for the celebration have been read, the novice is invited to approach the altar where some formal questioning takes place. When that is over he or she who is about to make profession reads aloud (so that all in the church can hear) the text which he or she has written out especially for this decisive moment. 'Let him write the document with his own hand',[1] is what St Benedict had said! Then, when what had been written has been read, the one who at this very moment makes profession signs this special chart and shows it to each one of those who are accepting him or her into their own community. It, then, is put where it, according to St Benedict himself, should be. 'Let him place it on the altar',[2] were his words! And so the one, who now has made profession, and the whole community which is accepting him or her, exchange the kiss of peace and, then, the Mass continues as, together, everyone gives thanks and praise to God who is accepting all.

* * *

The first of the three promises which a guest can hear the novice make is that which Benedictines call 'stability'. It often means to many people just a promise to remain in one particular place, that is, within the confines of the monastery in which profession has been made. But, since a lot of Benedictine monks and nuns will not, in fact, do that and, since from time to time they may be even told to go to somewhere else, a geographical defining of the term will not suffice. And yet, before we look for any other, let us recognise that a 'stability of place' deserves to be considered, too. Indeed, a Benedictine monk or nun, unlike the members of most Orders in the Church, is rooted in a very special way in his or her own monastery and, if that person has to travel to some other place, it can be, therefore, with a certain sense of coming 'home' that he, or she, will afterwards return. In this, the Benedictine monk or nun can often have a basic pattern of living, and perhaps an attitude to life which flows from it, which is not too dissimilar to that of many other people in the world.

However this 'stability' is not really to a place but to the people who are living there. With them the novice has begun a certain way of life and now that novice is declaring his or her desire to stay with them and, with their help, to persevere in such a life and in what it implies. That will, of course, demand a lot of social qualities which we must ponder later on. But, for the moment, let us simply note that once again we have a factor which unites the one who makes profession with so many others in the Church. Do we not all have families and friends? Do we not know that our own growth as individuals depends, in no small way, on the stability of our relationships with them? And, finally, do we not also know, what Benedictine monks and nuns explicitly express, that these relationships will only blossom as they should if they are rooted in that ultimate relationship which is the one we have with God and which he, constantly, is offering to us?

But is there any other way of understanding this stability? I would suggest there is. Perhaps, I could use here a story from the *Dialogues*. It tells us that St Benedict, when he was told about a hermit by the name of Martin who had chained himself to some great rock, sent him an urgent message. 'If thou be a servant of God let no chain or iron hold you but the chain of Christ,'[3] he said. And that advice was taken, we are told, and it was found to be both sensible and good.

But let us come a little closer to our time. There is a certain congregation of religious sisters who have chosen as their motto one short pregnant phrase from the letter of St Paul to the Ephesians. That quite newly-founded congregation is the Medical Missionaries of Mary and the motto which they chose, and which is always written on the notice-board in their own mother-house, is 'rooted and founded in love'.[4] Is that not also a true statement of stability? Indeed, I would suggest, it is the ultimate, and fundamental, one! All friendships and, particularly that one which we have with Christ can lead us more and more into the mystery of 'love' which is, itself, a synonym for God. Then, when we are well-rooted there, all that is worthwhile in our lives can grow. It may, perhaps, be relevant to add that both the foundress and the early members of that congregation stayed for some years at a Benedictine monastery before they had the opportunity to set up on their own.

* * *

The second promise which the novice makes is what the Rule calls 'conversatio morum'. This is frequently translated as 'conversion' but what those who witness a profession often hear is some interpretation of the term as in the formula: 'I promise to observe monastic life'. But, let us note that here again we find an element which can be relevant to many other people too. It is the recognition that the peace we seek will generally come through some particular way of living and that, if we want to have that peace, we have to learn how to accept that way of living, too. For some it may be the monastic one, for many others it may be the married or some form of single state. For almost everyone there surely will be some particular way of living, or of *conversatio*, to be accepted in their lives.

And yet this promise means, not only the acceptance of a certain way of life, but also the acceptance of that inner transformation which that way of living can, in its own way, facilitate. This second-level thought is also indicated in the Rule for it refers, not just to a conversion, but to stages of conversion, too. The new arrival, for example, is described as, 'coming to conversion'[5] which, as we have seen, can be interpreted as simply the acceptance of a certain, and in this case, the monastic way of life. But later, when the Rule has been presented and presumably fulfilled, the final chapter points the reader towards another and a further goal. 'For him who would hasten to the perfection of conversion,'[6] it begins and then goes on to indicate some authors who may be of help. But, here, what is proposed is, not a way of living but the climax of that personal conversion which occurs as one accepts the love and life of Christ. And as that happens one will make, to quote the Rule again: 'more and more progress into God',[7] who is, as we have noted, 'love'. But let us note that this *conversion process* is a possibility for everyone and not just for the Benedictine monk or nun!

* * *

We could say that these promises, whoever it may be that makes them, complement each other in their different emphases. The first, that of stability, concerns our roots and our identity and, therefore, the essential contribution which we make to other people's lives and which, in turn, they should be able to expect from us. The second promise, on the other hand, concerns our readiness to live a certain kind of life and, then, to let ourselves be totally transformed so that we can continue doing so with generosity and ease.

Esther de Waal, when she was speaking to a group about the Benedictine way of life, compared these promises to the components of a spiral staircase which she illustrated with a most impressive slide. A number of ascending steps were seen and they, as she explained, were symbols of the different and ever-better ways through which we can respond to God in all the changing circumstances of our lives. They were, in other words, the images of our 'conversion'. But, right down the centre of the picture, where the steps appeared to overlap, there was what seemed to be a central column and that symbolised, she said, that strong stability or rootedness which makes all adaptation to a changing world both possible and good. The picture was, as far as I can now remember, of a staircase in the church at Canterbury, where she had been living at the time. It was particularly apt because that very church, like many others of its age, would have been built by Benedictine monks whose lives were moulded by these very promises or vows.

* * *

But there is yet another promise which the one about to be professed must make. It is that of 'obedience' and, once again, we find a double-level operating here. It is, on one of these, the promise to obey the rules and regulations which make life in a community both possible and good. But, this promise is not just to people who surround us and who tell us to do this or that. It is to God himself who speaks to us through them. However, if we are to hear him properly we need to listen to much more than just to what a neighbour says. We need to be receptive to all kinds of signals and, not least, to those which come from deep within ourselves! What the disciple of St Benedict is, therefore, being urged to do is to develop a capacity for listening to a very subtle word which comes in different ways and, then, to learn how, like the cheerful giver,[8]to respond.

There is a point which may be worthwhile noting here. It is that in the Latin language *to obey* is similar, in sound and sense, to that word which in English is translated as 'to listen'. That seems to suggest that *to obey* presumes some kind of listening on our part. However, in the English language such a link is missing for, while *to obey* comes from the Latin, it has taken from its Saxon past the word which has become 'to listen' in our present day! Perhaps, however, we could argue that the verb 'to listen' does, at times, imply an element of some involvement, too, and one which is not always indicated, for example, by the verb 'to hear'! Do we not, for example, say of somebody at times: 'He heard me but he was not really listening!' Be that as it may, St Benedict would have us all increase our own capacity for listening to what God is saying in our lives so that his word may come alive in us and in all that we do.

Then we, in turn, will more effectively become his word to all those whom we meet!

* * *

The monk or nun who makes profession prays, and in a quite dramatic way, that he or she will be acceptable to God and that what is the deepest aspiration of the human heart will not be unfulfilled. With outstretched hands before the altar he or she intones, three times in all, the famous *Suscipe*. For those who are invited this can be a very moving moment and, perhaps, a moment which they will not easily forget.

The words which those who have assembled hear and which, in fact, have been passed down to us for generations now, are:

Suscipe me, Domine
secundum eloquium tuum
et vivam;
et non confundas me
ab expectatione mea.[9]

This, translated into English, is: 'Receive me, Lord, according to your word and I shall live. Do not disappoint me in my hope.' It is a cry for help. It is, however, a petition which the one who makes profession makes with confidence for this time what is wanted is, most surely, *in accordance with his word*.

But in this ceremony of profession, when the one who has expressed a resolution to be rooted, changed and open to the word,[10] has finished his, or her, own singing of this antiphon, the whole community begins to sing it, too. Indeed, in days to come it will sing these same words each time it has some reason to renew its promise and to give new sparkle to its hope. The individuals within it may, at other times, repeat them too and so may everybody who is present and, indeed, all others who, in some way, feel invited to make this same kind of personal commitment of their lives.

The Overflow

A guest is one who comes and stays awhile and then goes back to his or her own home. Some may, of course, return another time and some may like to count those monks or nuns who helped them in a special way among their more supportive friends. But it will always be within their own environment, wherever that may be, that their own contribution to the lives of others will most frequently be made. That contribution may, however, take a lot of different forms, according to the talents and the personality of each, but what we must consider here is that most fundamental contribution without which all others would be somehow incomplete. It is the overflow of peace into the lives of all those people whom, in their own situation, the departing guest will meet.

* * *

This seems to have been what occurred in Subiaco long ago. St Benedict spent all his energies at first on 'seeking God' alone but later, when some local people found him, he not only made them welcome, but provided what St Gregory calls 'spiritual food',[1] for them as well. He must, of course, have told them in their conversations who he was and why he lived the kind of life he did, for they must surely have enquired! But, then, he must have told them, too, about the God whom he had come to know and then, no doubt, about what they should do if they desired to find contentment in their lives. However, since 'the holy man cannot have taught otherwise than as he lived',[2] his teaching must have been more by example than by words and those who came to him must have received, not only new ideas, but also something of that Spirit which was animating him!

* * *

The portrait of St Benedict which we discover in the *Dialogues* is not unlike, in certain ways, that of the Benedictine abbot which is painted in the Rule. This latter, too, is one who has been 'found' by others for he is elected by them as their 'spiritual father', as the Rule says,

for the merit of his life.[3]

He, therefore, is a person who has found himself as one who has been called to teach and who must, therefore, give to his disciples and to all who come that 'spiritual food' which Benedict had given in his day. This teaching must, however, be provided by the quality of his own life more than by what he says and, in the Rule, he is reminded of that fact.

When anyone has received the name of abbot he ought to rule his disciples with a twofold teaching, displaying all goodnessand holiness by deeds and by words, *but by deeds rather than by words.*[4]

In other words, the abbot is to be a person who is calmly confident that, through whatever efforts he may make and through his very person when he is not making any, God's own Spirit can communicate itself to those who come to him.

*   *   *

Here let us look at one particular abbot who would have been moulded by the Benedictine Rule. He is the great St Bernard, that most influential person, not just in monastic circles, but throughout the whole of Europe, in his day. He preached, he wrote and, in his *Commentary on the Song of Songs*, he used a metaphor which can be valuable still. 'The man who is wise ... will see his life more like a reservoir than a canal,' he said and then, by way of explanation, added: 'the canal simultaneously pours out what it receives, the reservoir retains the water until it is filled, then discharges the overflow without loss to itself.'[5] He was referring to the preachers of his time and it is, certainly, important that such people do not just get up and pour forth any words that come into their mouths but that they share with those who listen to them thoughts which come out of a fullness in themselves. They must, in other words, be reservoirs! But it is also true that everyone who has received the love of God and has allowed it, then, to pour into each area of his or her own life will have a gift which can be shared with many other people, too. That was the case with Abbot Bernard and it can be in our own.

* * *

Another person who may help us here was also an important Abbot in those medieval days. He was concerned, especially, with building up community and with discerning the dynamics of relationships in terms of 'caritas' or love. His name was Aelred of Rievaulx.[6]

While he was abbot of that monastery he wrote a book which he entitled *Speculum Caritatis*, or *The Mirror of Charity*, to use its English name. It is about the way that we ought to relate to one another, which, for him, was a reflection of the mystery of the Trinity itself! While everyone remains distinct, each can contribute to the lives of others and so share with them a life which is itself unique!

St Aelred was, however, very much aware that to relate to others can be difficult at times. He knew that there are people whom we do not naturally like and that we, consequently, have to make some effort to accept them as they are. Of course, there are those other people whom we find attractive but for them we often have to make an effort too. In their case it may be to let them have their necessary space! The aim, however, in both situations is the same. It is to make each person welcome but in such a way that they will, on the one hand, benefit from their relationship with us and, on the other, find a freedom in themselves. St Aelred's ultimate advice for realising such a wonderful ideal was simply that we all should keep on finding God within the context of our lives and, then, to:

    gather all the world
    into our hearts
    to share in our own peace.[7]

In that peace they will surely find that combination of both freedom and encouragement which they themselves require.

* * *

To jump, now, from the Middle Ages to our present century, let me introduce a friend who studied with me many years ago. He was a very placid, Oriental, Benedictine monk and we discussed a lot of things together. Then, one day, he shared a thought which I have shared with many people since and which is worthwhile sharing once again. It was that, in our dealings with the people whom we meet, we should 'first win them to ourselves and, then, direct them on to God', and I remember still the way he pointed, with his finger, first, towards himself and, then, across his shoulder, to the Unseen Presence which, he obviously knew, was there. It was a lesson which I have remembered all these years and, if he was referring, at that moment, to the way that one ought to relate to students in a secondary school, I now know that his message has far wider applications too.

In every situation, therefore, we can be a beneficial presence in the lives of others. Then, like John the Baptist (in whose honour Benedict himself had built a shrine[8]), we too can point the way to One who knows them better than we do ourselves. Indeed, when somebody is ready to move on, the best way to express the love of God for him or her may be, precisely, by our willingness to let that person go! But, if that has to happen, we can always be assured that, while they seem to go, we will be, in the best way, with them still!

* * *

Let me conclude this chapter with a comment on a story which we all know very well. It is the Gospel story of the 'Visitation' and it merits mention here because it was adopted by that congregation of religious sisters which I mentioned earlier as an expression of their missionary goal. It tells us, as we know, how Mary went with haste to help Elizabeth who was with child and, for the founder of that congregation, that enthusiastic gesture seemed to symbolise what she desired her followers to do: to offer their own sympathetic services to the women of Nigeria! But in the very story of the Visitation it is said that, well before such midwifery assistance had begun, Elizabeth herself received a very special gift. 'When she heard the greeting of Mary ... she was filled with the Holy Spirit'[9] Does that not suggest that even the most ordinary gestures of each day can have at times extra-ordinary value, too? Does it not mean that, if the life of God is growing in us as it should, the very act of greeting someone can become for those who have the eyes to see, not just a friendly gesture, but a sign of something more? Indeed, through every-thing we say and do, and even by our very presence in the lives of others, God's own Spirit can reach out and they can be, per-haps irrevocably, changed!

Part Three

The Garden Shed

Chapter four is not a bad place to begin if one wants to explore the moral and the social teaching of St Benedict. It is a chapter which contains a lot of simple do's and don'ts which he himself obtained from other writers and, in many cases, from the Sacred Scriptures, too. They all are bunched together here. However, while some commentators like to say that there are certain groupings in the list and even that there is a pattern which weaves itself throughout the chapter as a whole, the image given by the author is that of a lot of tools stored in a garden shed! The title of the chapter, therefore, could, perhaps, be re-translated, as 'the tools or instruments for working well'! However, as we now approach that 'shed' and enter it, we will begin to notice that, while each tool has a purpose of its own and can be used when the appropriate occasion comes, St Benedict has changed the shape of some to make them even easier to handle and he has included, too, some new ones of his own.

* * *

This chapter opens with the double-precept of the Lord:

> In the first place, to love the Lord God with all one's heart, all one's soul and all one's strength, then, one's neighbour as oneself.[1]

These are, of course, the 'great commandments' which, according to the Gospel, should suggest in every situation what we ought to do.[2] However, we can also take them to assess the value of what is already done! In that case we may see that some of our own deeds and words and even thoughts had not in any way been influenced by them in any way at all! But much more frequently, perhaps, as we examine our behaviour we will see that, even when we have done nothing wrong, the loving Spirit which is in us may have been a little weak!

St Benedict, as far as we can see, looked forward to a time when love in his disciples would become so strong that it would flow, without impediment, through everything they did. For instance, at the end of chapter seven (which concludes his Spiritual Charter[3]) he refers to that perfected love which, having banished every crippling fear, will let us do the good things we are doing 'without labour'[4] and with ease. However, he must have another reason for including here, as chapter four (and his great Spiritual Charter) starts, these great commandments of the Lord. Is it because he wants to say: love is not just the goal of Christian life; it is its origin, as well? Quite probably! In any case, to start by loving God and neighbour (both are inter-twined) is, certainly, the best way to ensure that Love itself will grow and, thereby, simplify our all-too-often complicated and disintegrated lives.

This love is very powerful and transforming but it is itself a mystery we will never fully comprehend. However, the Nigerian who broke the word into its different letters and explained what each one meant, was possibly identifying it as well as anyone could reasonably wish. If you 'Leave Off the Various Evils' in your life, he said (although he did not entertain me with a list), all that is left is Love! I was intrigued. I even thought of how we filtered water in those parts before we dared to drink. But, in my heart I knew already that what he had said was true. Love comes from God himself, indeed it is his Spirit, and when it is flowing through us, minus those impurities which we can easily add, it will not only nourish our own lives but irrigate to some extent the lives of other people, too.

* * *

The next 'tools' which are mentioned in the list in chapter four have all, with one small change,[5] been borrowed from the famous Ten Commandments. They, however, reach a certain climax when St Benedict concludes with what is, frequently, referred to as 'the Golden Rule'. It is, as given to us here:

> not to do to another what one would not have done to one-self.[6]

It should, perhaps, be noted that this version, which is found in Jewish, Greek and Roman sources, speaks of what one should

not do. So, being negative, it is unlike the more demanding version which is given to us in the Sermon on the Mount.[7]
However it is most important, too. Indeed it could be thought of
as that basic rule of conduct without which no civilised society,
and certainly no Christian group, could ever manage to exist.

But, here let us adapt this Golden Rule in order to express an insight which those who are sensitive to people and their needs
will readily endorse. Let us interpret it as saying, therefore:
do not do to another what you would not have done to yourself *if you were as that other person actually is.*
That should not only urge us to exclude those words and deeds
which would be disagreeable to everyone, but also to avoid all
those which could be hurtful to the one to whom we are relating
at the time. St Benedict himself would have approved of this
amendment for he was himself a person who was very much
aware that everyone is not the same.[8] Indeed, if we take what he
wrote as mirroring himself, he was a person who was always
ready to 'adapt himself to many dispositions' or, to quote another sentence to 'accommodate himself to all'.[9]

But, here, are we not moving towards a sensitivity to people
which is able to facilitate, not just avoiding what might hurt
them, but responding to their needs, as well? A positive interpretation of the Golden Rule inevitably surfaces for those who
want to live committed Christian lives!

* * *

When one reads through the list of instruments in chapter four
one notices that they refer, not only to the way that one ought to
behave, but sometimes to one's inner dispositions, too. Thus,
while the dictum: 'not to yield to anger'[10] may suggest behaviour which should be avoided, the prescriptions:
not to nurse a grudge,
not to hold guile in one's heart[11]
refer quite clearly to an attitude, as well. Perhaps, the reader of a
rule for monks will be surprised that anger, grudge and guile
are even thought of as a possibility at all but human groupings,
be they of monastic personnel or not, are fundamentally the
same! The urging of the Rule in this connection, therefore, can
be applicable to us all. It is not only: 'not to make a feigned

peace',[12] but to 'make peace with one's adversary before the sun goes down.'[13] St Benedict would obviously like us to initiate the process which can overcome unpleasantness as quickly as we can. That is, he seems to say, the best way to transcend those barriers which can so easily arise within relationships. It also guarantees for those who are estranged, and possibly for those around them too, the advent of another and, potentially at least, more satisfying day!

* * *

St Benedict, however, does not think about morality as if it were a merely private enterprise, but always as behaviour in connection with the person and the power of Christ. Thus, for example, when he says that we ought to deny ourselves it is:

to follow Christ.[14]

This self-denial is related to accepting him, not only as a guide as we continue on our way through life, but frequently as model or exemplar, too!

However, the expression 'to deny oneself' deserves some further explanation here. It does not mean that we have to adopt some kind of masochistic attitude towards ourselves or fail to see and to appreciate the goodness which is in us, even now. It merely indicates, as does the Gospel verse which it is echoing, that there is in us all a superficial, less well-anchored 'self', which during life needs to be rooted in the deeper and substantial 'self', (and so controlled) if we are to develop as we should. In other words there are in each of us two different 'selves', and it is only one of them which needs, at times, to be restrained! Psychologists may call these two parts of ourselves by other names but, here, what we can say is that the deeper part, the deeper 'self', the one which is not to be thwarted but encouraged, will, as it develops, mirror more and more distinctly him who is our guide and model, Jesus Christ himself. In doing so, it will, moreover, influence and tame the other self, as well.

There are two more occasions when there is a reference to Christ in this conglomerated list of chapter four. The first is in the often-quoted phrase which tells us that we should:

prefer nothing to the love of Christ.[15]

The second is inserted by St Benedict himself into the list he had received. It says that one should:

pray for one's enemies in the love of Christ.[16]

This latter may remind us of the time when he himself, according to St Gregory, not only did not nurture enmity against an envious and persecuting priest, but grieved when that same person was precipitously killed.[17]However, while the first phrase could suggest the love *we have for Christ* or that which *he now has for us,* the second one is not ambiguous at all. It clearly means his love for us for it is only in accepting that, that we will learn to love all others and forgive those who have hurt us in some way.

Christ is, in all such situations, the essential key to true morality and to community development, as well.

* * *

A little more than half-way down the list there are two instruments which are quite different from the rest! They do not talk about behaviour, nor of inner dispositions, but about a way of understanding life. The first one says that one ought:

to attribute to God, and not to self, whatever good one sees in oneself.[18]

The second is the counter-view:

to recognise that the evil is one's own doing, and to impute it to oneself.[19]

That makes one think! In fact, I can recall the first time that I read those sentences and how they gradually opened up for me a new perspective which allowed me to see everything for what they really are. I know that people sometimes feel that these two statements are quite disconcerting for, they say, 'it is unpleasant to be told that, after all the effort which we make, it is, not we, but God who must be praised when we succeed while, on the other hand, if we do not succeed, the fault has always to be ours!' And yet the more one thinks about these sentences the more one comes to realise that what they mean is actually true.

The second one, if we can take it first, refers to the results of human selfishness and greed. Such evils, unlike purely natural disasters, come from us! Of course, we could plead that they come from that unanchored part of us which has not been transformed within the goodness of our deeper selves but, even so, we cannot say that we have, therefore, no responsibility at all. Of course, we can proclaim that God is good and that he is a loving father who accepts us as we are but that is not sufficient reason to ignore completely all the imperfections in ourselves. Indeed, it can be salutary for us to admit our faults and to acknowledge that, although we welcome it, we, certainly, do not deserve God's generous and rectifying love.

As for the first proposal, that the good we see within ourselves should be attributed to God, that also must be true. If God is infinitely good, as Scripture says he is, there cannot be another goodness which is not, in some way, emanating from him and included in his own! And so, we must conclude that any good which there may be in us and any good which we may consequently do is always the result of his own Spirit working in our own. Indeed the Scriptures tell us that it is in him that we all live and move and have our very being.[20] What St Benedict would have us do is simply to acknowledge that!

* * *

One final thought! It is that all the good that we can do is to be done, according to this chapter, in the place where we reside:

> The workshop wherein we shall diligently execute all these tasks is the enclosure of the monastery and stability in the community.[21]

For the monk or nun, the monastery, of course, is where the art of Christian living will be learnt. For other people other places will be their 'enclosure' and where their 'stability' will generally be. But, for them all, the same temptation may arise, that is to think that it would be much easier to live a Christian life if only one could go to somewhere else! The far-off hills are green! St Benedict, however, seems to think that they are seldom so. It is, he seems to say, where you belong that you can blossom, not in some utopia of which you tend to dream.

And yet that very dream can have a value, too. It may be the anticipated image of a world which, though we will not ever find it here, will in the future come!

The Ballet

Comments made by people who have been to a monastic meal are often interesting. For most of them it is a very different experience to any that they ever had before and so, if they say anything at all, it often will be only to express surprise at certain, relatively simple things. For example, some may comment on the way the tables are arranged, that is: along each side, so that all those who come to eat will have to face each other but across an empty space! Some others may remark that they did not expect to have to eat in silence but that, when they realised that somebody was reading to them while they ate, they settled and discovered that the whole experience was quite relaxing after all! However, there are also those who say that they are fascinated by the movement of the monks who serve! 'It was impressive,' one observed when it was over while another, with exuberance, exclaimed, 'It was like going to a ballet'! That was a comparison that one could not forget.

* * *

For readers who have never had the opportunity to be at a monastic meal, it might be useful to reflect a little on its meaning and on its importance for our lives. If it, as that enthusiastic guest exclaimed, can be considered as a kind of 'ballet', it is one which is constructed on a very ordinary need: the need for daily food. However, in the Rule, the meal is thought of as an opportunity, not for the hungry to sit down and eat, as we might be inclined to think, but for the ones who have been asked to serve!

> Let the brethren serve one another and let no one be excused
> from the kitchen service, unless because of sickness or be-
> cause he is involved in some business of importance.[1]

Those who, like the Cellarer,[2] had much to do, and so were serving the community some other way, were not obliged to serve at table, too. But it is clear that this particular service was considered so important, and so useful for the servers, that St Benedict desired as many of his followers as possible to have the opportunity to do what it entailed.

It could, perhaps, be noted here that, when the Rule was being written, 'kitchen service' would have meant, not just the serving in the refectory, but all the preparation and the cooking of the meal, as well. Today, that 'kitchen' part may have been frequently hived off to other people who, perhaps, can cook a better meal than any of the monks! (However, that itself could be considered as an application of the principle contained in the remark that: 'only those who edify their hearers should be asked to read!'[3]) In any case, in every Benedictine monastery that I have visited the old tradition of monks serving one another in the refectory itself has been retained and it is one which many say contains enormous value, too. Indeed, I can recall one old professor-monk requesting, on the day that he retired, that it should never be abandoned for, he claimed, it teaches more than he himself, in all his years, had ever managed in the class-room to achieve! It teaches those who do the serving how to notice what their neighbours need and, if their serving can in truth be called a 'ballet', it may also teach them to provide what is required in a manner which is gracious and acceptable to all.

* * *

This serving in the refectory is more than just a job. It is a way of practising that charity which is encouraged by the Rule.[4] However, it is also more than just one exercise of that great virtue which St Benedict would have us practise in all other situations, too.[5] Because this service is a kind of ritual (a ballet it was called!) it is or can become a living sign of what life as a whole is meant to be. Indeed, we can say even more! We can say that it is a sign which can occasion 'an increase of charity'[6] in those who charitably serve.

Today, we need such salutary signs! The world in which we live can often make us think a lot about our own advancement and

ourselves and not too much about the person and the needs of
others whom we meet. The Rule would make us do the opposite. Indeed a sentence in a final chapter reads:

> Let no one follow what he judges good for himself but rather
> what is good for the other.[7]

That, of course, may seem to some as taking it too far. There are
occasions, they will say, when it is right to do what seems good
for oneself and Benedict would probably agree. Is not the whole
thrust of his Rule to guarantee that our essential needs are always catered for? It is within that context, therefore, that he tells
his own disciples that they must not let their lives through selfishness become a counter-sign to what they ought to be.

* * *

Since charity begins with God, who is according to the Scriptures
'love', those who desire to practise it will do so best when they
are rooted well in him. Thus, in the Rule, it is laid down that
those who are about to start their weekly service in the refectory
should come before the whole community and ask the Lord for
help. A psalm-verse, which is now the opening verse for most of
the official prayer-times of the Church, was stipulated for them,
too.

> O God, come to my aid;
> O Lord, make haste to help me.[8]

Today, some monasteries have not retained this custom but,
where it occurs, it can be quite impressive to observe. However,
whether it is kept or not, it surely is important to remember that,
not only in the refectory, but in the whole of life, this help from
God is always needed if we really are to serve.

There is a story in the *Dialogues* which illustrates how much we
who are often weak can need the power of God's own loving
Spirit if we are to serve. It tells us that a monk, who was of noble
birth, was murmuring in his heart when he had been requested
to perform a simple, if a lowly, task. St Benedict, who was aware
of this, said simply:

> sign yourself, brother, sign yourself.[9]

It was his way of coaxing the reluctant server to reflect on his behaviour in the sight of God but also to remember who it is that
he himself had promised to accept in life as model and as guide!

The Rule itself has its own way of emphasising who it is that servers ought to imitate. It says that those who are about to start their week of serving in the refectory, and those who have completed it as well, should wash the feet of all the others who are there![10] Today, we do not normally wash people's feet except, of course, on Holy Thursday in the church. But we, perhaps, have other gestures of our own which can, at times, become a sign, not of some passing wish to please, but of a total giving of ourselves. Indeed, we need such special gestures and we need to ponder and admire them, too, if God's unbounded goodness is to reach out through us to the people whom we serve.

* * *

When we have served and done all that we should, we should, as well, give thanks to God because without his hidden help we would not have been able to accomplish what we did. St Benedict, who was convinced of that, required his own disciples, when their period of serving in the refectory was over, to come out before the whole community and publicly express their gratitude in prayer. Again, he had a psalm-verse which he was prepared to recommend and so they would repeat:

Blessed are you, Lord God,
for you have helped me
and consoled me too.[11]

This was, of course, for them a small, and yet symbolic, application of the recommended 'tool': to recognise the good which flows through us as coming, in the last analysis, from God and to attribute it to him![12] But it is one which, in so many situations, we can all too easily forget!

However, in the situation which is mentioned in the Rule the whole community is asked to say this psalm-verse which the servers have already said and so the meaning of the ceremony grows. It now articulates the gratitude, not just of those who have completed their allotted task, but also of the monks who have received the gifts which ultimately came, not from the servers, but from God. Is there some echo here of what was said about that very first community, that:

they partook of food with glad and generous hearts, praising God and having favour with all the people?[13]

Perhaps! In any case, it does express what every Christian gathering should be: a people full of gratefulness to God and of attractive and contagious praise!

* * *

St Benedict does not say much about the Mass. Indeed, apart from some remarks about receiving the Communion[14] and the possibility and place of priests[15] in the community itself, he almost totally ignores it. One could, therefore, be excused from thinking that it must have played an unimportant part in his own way of understanding and appreciating life. Yet, as the years went by, the celebration of the Mass became for many monasteries a central part, not only of their weekly round, but of each day as well. And so it has remained. It, therefore, seems to me that at this juncture we should try to understand it, not perhaps as we have done till now, but through the general perspective of the Rule and, in particular, through what is said about the comparable ritual which takes place in the refectory.

The celebration of the Mass is, certainly, a ritual! To say that it is also something of a 'ballet' may sound strange, especially to those who are accustomed only to the Mass as it is celebrated in a quiet country church. It may, however, sound a little more appropriate to those who are familiar with the more developed liturgies of larger churches or, perhaps, of Benedictine monasteries. In all such places there can be a lot of people taking part and moving, in accordance with a worked-out plan, around the altar-area. At times, though in some places more than others, one may also find a form of dance or even of some quite sophisticated choreography!

But let us concentrate on that part of the Mass which does seem to be mentioned in the Rule. I am referring to the moment of communion when participants receive the Sacrament itself. This is a very sacred moment but it is much more than the occasion for developing a personal relationship with God. It is the moment when God can remind us that there are a lot of other people in the church and that we are related to each one of them, as well.

In such a context gestures are important. For example, when the moment for communion comes, each one receives the sacrament from someone else and anyone who is a eucharistic minister can give it to some others, too. This giving and receiving, which we often take for granted, should, however, be considered an essential part of our communion rite. It sums up for us, as we share the Sacrament itself, the many other givings and receivings which make up our human lives. But, on the other hand, these gestures in the church can be a challenge for us, too! They can remind us that we must not let our lives become frustrated by 'self-service thinking' and that we should learn how to receive with gratitude the gifts which others bring and, in return, to give with growing generosity to those who are in need.

The communion rite would have expressed this giving and receiving more completely when the Rule was being written than it does today. In Rome itself, the Pope, when he had said the Eucharistic or Thanksgiving Prayer, would have gone to his *cathedra*, or throne, in order to receive the Sacrament from someone else. In other words, he did not merely take it as a celebrant will do today. Indeed, according to the writer of a recent work:

> the general rule in communion rites right up to through the Middle Ages, in both East and West, was that communion is not just taken but given and received.[16]

We have moved far from that position and the understanding which occasioned it but I suspect that it was nearer to the thinking of St Benedict than, often, is our own.

The Mass is, therefore, able to become the celebration of our mutual dependence and concern. It can, moreover, help us to appreciate the giving and receiving of each day within the greater and enabling context of the love which we receive from Christ who gave himself for us. It is that love which we are called to share with one another every day.

Fine Tuning

In Africa I had a radio which I used every night to get the London News. A few of us would sit around it and, with great attention, I would turn that extra knob which was for what is called 'fine-tuning'. Then, the distant voice of the announcer would be heard, and though at times it still could be a little indistinct, we were kept fairly well in touch with what was happening in the world and, sometimes, even made aware of what we ought to do ourselves.

Life is at times like that! God, who can speak to us in many ways, seems to accept that we will often have to make an extra effort if we are to hear him when what he is asking us to do is, not just unattractive but demanding, too. He knows, in other words, that at such moments we will have to manage some 'fine-tuning' of ourselves!

The Rule, which would have us excel in doing this, refers to certain situations where that extra effort must quite frequently be made if certain types of people, to whom Benedict himself was very well attuned, are to receive from us the sympathetic treatment they require.

* * *

St Benedict was conscious of those people in his own community who could be over-burdened and, at times, weighted down. When referring, for example, to the Cellarer, who (as his names implies) had charge of all the monastery's provisions and who, therefore, could have many things to do, he urged that he would also have whatever help an over-busy situation might require. But let us note his very words for they reveal what was in this his ultimate concern. He wrote:

if the community be a large one let helpers be given him so
that, with their assistance, he may fulfil, with a quiet mind,
the charge that has been committed to him.[1]

That he should enjoy 'a quiet mind'! That phrase shows just how
much St Benedict desired to help and it is one which finds an
echo in a later chapter when, referring to the kitchen servers, he
says much the same.

The weak should have help provided for them, that they may
not perform their office with sadness.[2]

St Benedict did not want people to be sad! But, obviously, he desired his readers to acquire an equal sensitivity to those around
them and to learn how to respond to what may often only be a
silent plea for some assistance in some difficult or heavy task.

* * *

St Benedict was also conscious of the needs both of the elderly
and of the very young. Although his major source did not refer
to them at all,[3] he obviously felt that they deserved a special
chapter in his Rule. Of course, while we accept as natural the fact
that some monks can be old, we can be quite surprised to hear
that children would have been admitted to a monastery at all.
However, that was the accepted custom of the time and, maybe,
we could say in its defence that in a very troubled age a Benedictine monastery may have appeared to many as a safe and
even beneficial place for any growing child. But, be that as it
may, the point which most concerns us here is that St Benedict,
not only recognised that both the young and old have special
needs, but that he wanted to ensure that they were satisfied, as
well. He had, indeed, a gentle and attentive soul!

Care for the old and for the very young can be, however, quite
demanding. They require attention and some carers may, at
times, have other things to do, as well. Of course, St Benedict
would always want, as we have seen, an over-burdened carer to
have help but, on the other hand, he was prepared to nudge his
followers, especially no doubt those who were most involved,
towards a spirit of compassionate concern. 'Let there be constant
compassion for their weakness,'[4] he declared and, just a little
later in that chapter (which, in fact, has only six or seven lines)
he repeated that desire.[5] Compassion, therefore, was for him the

virtue which should carry our attention and allow it to become effective in the way that we respond.

* * *

St Benedict was much concerned about the welfare of those members of his own community who were infirm.

Before all things
and above all things
care must be taken of the sick.[6]

Indeed, not only did he recognise that those who are not well need extra things, like special food,[7] but he desired them all to have facilities which were not common at the time. For example, he decreed that they should have 'a special room'[8] and also 'an attendant',[9] who presumably would not be also occupied with many other things. That was the start of what would grow into the more developed hospital and health amenities which we enjoy today.

St Benedict, however, did insist that those who were unwell should not abuse the system nor annoy those serving them with their 'unreasonable demands.[10] Yet, even if that were to happen, he appreciated that the sick are sick and that the greater obligation, therefore, is on those who serve. In other words, there was in him a listening heart which may have helped him to discern the true needs of the sick and at the same time made him always ready to respond.

One phrase, however, in his chapter on the sick requires a special comment here. It is the one which says that they, the sick, should realise that it is for 'the honour of God'[11] that they are being served. That should, according to St Benedict, make them reduce their more 'unreasonable demands'! But such a thought can be a little disconcerting, too. It would be more consoling, many say, and consequently much more healing too if they were helped to feel that they were being served because they had a value in themselves! However, it was hardly the intention of St Benedict to overlook, much less deny, that most important fact. It is more likely that he wanted those who served the sick 'to honour God' so that the very needs of those whom they were serving would, with even greater clarity, be seen and that they would be always truly honoured in themselves.

* * *

St Benedict was attentive to the needs of others but, particularly, of the poor. The age in which he lived was not a peaceful one for armies frequently traversed the land and caused inevitable harm. The poor, and those who then became so, must have often gravitated to such places as his own for food or some kind of support. At times, such people must have been a nuisance, too, especially if the community itself was struggling to survive. But, even if that was the case, St Benedict insisted that such people should not be ignored. Indeed, he nudged his followers to give them extra care.

The chapter on receiving guests, unlike the one which was its major source,[12] contains a special reference to those who can so easily be overlooked. It says that:

> in the reception of poor people ... special attention should be shown ... for the fear which the rich inspire is enough of itself to secure them honour.[13]

Here is a perceptive comment on our human tendency to gravitate towards those people whom we feel may help us most and, at the same time, an encouragement to welcome those who seem least likely to do anything for us at all. This counter-preference is echoed later when 'the old man at the gate', that is the porter, is instructed what to do. 'As soon as anybody knocks or a poor person comes, let him answer "Deo Gratias"',[14] St Benedict declared! Does this not seem to say that when we welcome those who come, and in a special way the poor, we honour God himself who is, in some way, present in them, too?

There is a story in the *Dialogues* which tells us how St Benedict insisted that a poor man, who had begged for oil, should get some, even though it was the last drop in the house.[15] However, even when the poor have need of food and drink and clothes and oil they can have other needs as well. They can need, for example, to discover, or to rediscover, their own self-esteem and the awareness that, in spite of everything, they have a value in themselves. We all can help them to discover that, at least by recognising their essential dignity and, then, by treating them with genuine respect. The author of the Rule, however, seems to think that we can, sometimes, even do a little more!

One of the tools for living well which he has hanging for us in his Garden Shed is

re-create the poor.[16]

It is for those occasions when we find that we can help them to accept the fact that deep down they are good … when we can help them to appreciate a little more that they have been created in the image of the God who is himself 'all-good' … and when we can, in some way, make it possible for them to grow a little more into his likeness, too![17] When that occurs we are participating in the work of God himself who wants those very people to attain the fullness of that life for which, according to the Scriptures, he himself created them.

* * *

St Benedict was conscious of the people who had special needs. But he saw more in them than just some individuals who happened to be over-burdened, sick or poor. He saw in them the presence and the mystery of Christ!

For a moment, let us check this statement with some comments in the Rule. There, Benedict, when speaking of the sick, says that they should be treated well:

because in them Christ can be truly served![18]

A little later, when referring to receiving guests, he adds that those who come with nothing are to get a special welcome for:

in them is Christ more truly welcomed![19]

He does not declare explicitly that Christ is present in the over-burdened and the old and in the very young but, since he does say that 'we are all one in Christ'[20] we can presume that he perceived his presence in those other people, too.

The Christ who is in all these people is, of course, Christ in his yet unglorified humanity! Thus, through our helping and accepting those who are in need, we are in some way helping Christ himself to grow! But, as that happens, through the very service which we give, has not the presence of that Christ an opportunity to grow within ourselves, as well?

A Dream

St Benedict had a dream! It was a marvellous dream! It was a dream about a whole community of people who were sharing all they had and in which there was nobody who would declare that anything was only his! It was a dream which had been dreamt by others who had lived before him and, as he reflected on the words of one of them, he must have been impressed for later, when he wrote his Rule, they influenced his own.

> Let all things be common to all nor let anyone say that anything is his own.[1]

And so, like Luke, the author of the Acts of the Apostles who had hoped that Christian groupings would become what true communities should be, St Benedict desired his own disciples to become the same.

However, he desired that his disciples would, not only share all that they had, but that they would be able to accept the fact that each did not require the same! In practice this would mean that any distribution of what was available for all would have to take into consideration the requirements of each one. In order to provide a Scriptural authority for this humane, but easily ignored, ideal St Benedict decided to include another sentence from the Acts of the Apostles and to use it to support his own request.

> Let us follow Scripture: 'distribution was made to each according to the needs of each'.[2]

Then, later, when referring to such things as food and drink and clothing he provided us with an example by insisting that each one should get what each in fact required.[3]

The text which I have quoted here, however, may suggest another which goes back to very early times. I am referring now to one which says that, on their journey to the Promised Land, the

Chosen People were content to let each one collect the quantity of Manna which that person needed for that day.[4] So, as we read the Rule of Benedict and keep those texts in mind, we may feel that on our own journey through this life we, too, should have that same unruffled toleration for each other which is intimated there. In other words we should not envy those who have to get a little more than we receive ourselves nor should we over-estimate our own importance just because a need in us is being recognised.[5] Instead, like Benedict himself we should be quietly convinced that, if we all could only have a generous, uncalculating attitude, our own communities would have a greater opportunity to grow.

However, Benedict was also well aware that dreams are only dreams! Indeed, the author of the Acts of the Apostles, whom he echoes, was aware that even his description of the first community of Christians in Jerusalem was not completely true! Does he not also tell us that a couple, Ananias and Sapphira, while pretending to share everything, kept back a portion for themselves?[6] Does he not also say that in the bosom of that first community there was a group which had good reason to complain because their widows were neglected in the daily distribution of what was available for all?[7] St Benedict would certainly have noted that (indeed he mentions Ananias and Sapphira in another place[8]) but he knew from his personal experience as well that human nature frequently falls short of what it can attain. He, therefore, must have felt, as did St Luke himself, that if a spirit of true sharing is to grow in a community at all, it is essential to keep on proclaiming and admiring that ideal!

* * *

About sharing on a deeper level not much seems, at first, to be suggested in the Rule. St Benedict was mostly interested in organising life so that each individual could find his inner peace and, therefore, God himself from whom that peace had come. However, in the final chapters he acknowledges a little more that his disciples must relate to one another, too. He may not say too much about what this entails but he refers to three essential elements which must be always present if relationships are to develop as they should. They are the elements of love, of genuine respect and of a willingness to do what is required.

Concerning 'love', St Benedict expresses what is both a very general desire and a most demanding wish. 'Let them practice charity with a pure love',[9] he says and that, while almost platitudinous, deserves some comment here. It says, by implication, that our charity can be in fact 'impure' and that, of course, is true for motives in our lives, as we all know, are often mixed if not, indeed, confused. We have, however, noted that a 'perfect love' is something to which one aspires, though with the certain hope that, with the help of God, it can be finally attained![10] It is, in other words, a goal but it is also the initial step, as we have seen when looking at those tools which were provided for us in the famous Garden Shed.[11] All this implies that we must pray each day to God, who is all-love, and welcome him into each one of our relationships so that, once started, they will all be able to develop as they should!

Concerning 'genuine respect', St Benedict is very practical indeed! He does not speculate about the dignity of every individual but, hinting at the ordinary situations which we can encounter every day, he says:
let them (that is, his disciples) give each other precedence.[12]
Already in his Rule he had said something similar but, then, it was that junior members should respect and honour those who were their seniors in monastic life.[13] Here, he transcends such hierarchical concerns! Respect and honour are to be exhibited to everyone no matter who or what they are! This may not always be a quality of our contemporary world, but, without honour and respect and even reverence, how can the love which we should have for one another ever have a chance to grow?

Concerning 'willingness to do what is required', St Benedict encouragingly advises:
let them vie in paying obedience to each other.[14]
This does not mean that they should try to beat each other in this virtue as if life itself was some kind of a competition. On the contrary, it means that if one is inclined to think of being good in terms of points or marks which one may get, it would be better

to consider others and to do as much as possible for them. It means allowing our own sensitivity to grow so that we will be able to discern the needs of those whom God has brought along our path and, then, to note how, with his help, we can most suitably respond. This may involve our doing something for some person which that person may require or simply saying what another needs to hear or, equally important, our retreating so that somebody can find the necessary space that he or she requires. In every case our willingness to do what is required will make it possible for each relationship to grow to the extent and in the way it should.

* * *

It is a dream.

Some years ago, while waiting for a friend, I found a folder which contained the picture of a person with a partially completed jig-saw as a background to her head! Beneath, there was the caption: 'Have you found your place?' I was quite fascinated at the time and, later, when I had departed, and, in fact, gone overseas, I kept on thinking of that picture and about what it implied. Of course, one could say that it simply meant that all of us are, somehow, part of some great all-embracing plan. But, as I drove along a high-way in Nigeria, it seemed to me to be suggesting something more!

It seemed to be suggesting that, if we are to discover our position in the picture which is life, we must discover who we really are! To put that into Bible-language we could say that each of us needs to discover his or her true name![15] And so, as I reflected on those somewhat introspective thoughts, these words began to come together in my mind:

> Little pieces,
> all alike,
> yet none are quite the same;

> Little pieces,
> all together;
> each must find its special name!

To work out our relationship with all the people in our lives, however, may be difficult at times. Some we can like and we can even feel that they are very similar to us in certain ways. But, then, we can discover that the most important thing that we can do for them is to allow them to have space! They are like pieces of a jig-saw puzzle which, although we want to join them to the one which we are holding in our hands, have been, in fact, intended for another and more distant place! Then, there are those which we can easily ignore until some situation makes us realise that they should be brought closer and, perhaps, quite near! The trouble with this image is, of course, that life, unlike the picture on the jig-saw, keeps on changing all the time! The image seemed, however, at that moment to suggest a truth which does endure and, so, I stopped the car, took out my pen and wrote:

> Little pieces,
> joined to others
> but in different ways;
>
> Little pieces
> of a picture
> which a Patient Hand displays.

A Patient Hand! It seemed to me as I continued driving on that high-way that, just as the picture on a jig-saw has been planned by some designer long before we start assembling it, so, too, the pattern of our own inter-twining lives is known to a Designer all the time that we are struggling to discover what it is. Indeed, when for a while we seem to get it right, do we not often feel a need to give thanks to the Lord because a spiritual instinct in us keeps on saying that the picture which is coming into focus is much more his Work of Art than it can ever be considered ours! There may, of course, be other moments when we wonder what is really happening! But, to quote again the Letter to the Romans, God, who can surprise us, can, in his own way, bring all things unto good.[16]

> Little pieces
> play their part
> in a plan that is not theirs;

Little pieces
made to struggle
for a dream their Maker shares.

Little pieces! That is all we are! Little pieces made to struggle.
Yes, that often is the case! But, somehow, something in us keeps
repeating that, because God is in charge of everything, all can
and will be well!

A Hospital of Sorts!

St Benedict presents his readers with a very high ideal. It is, as we have seen, no less than to attain that love of which the Gospels speak! To reach that goal, however, one requires not only time and energy, but frequently the grace to overcome a lot of stumbles – and, perhaps, some disappointing falls, as well!

St Benedict gave those who wished to undertake this journey much advice. He gave them for example, all those well-tried maxims which have been collected into chapter four (that garden shed collection) and, throughout the other chapters of his Rule, he offered and elaborated on some more. But most importantly he urged them all to keep on serving one another as they travel and, as we have noted in the chapter just completed, he began to share with them some aspects of his dream.

However, when we take all that he said to heart, we can discover what his first disciples seem to have discovered, too. It is that we require, not only words however wise, but extra 'vitamins' as well if we are to continue struggling towards the summit and that, sometimes, we may need some form of medication, too!

* * *

The Rule, which keeps in mind a whole community, refers to situations in which faults or failings of one individual may cause some inconvenience, not just to another person (which it may), but to the total group. Thus, for example, we can find a chapter-heading which refers to:

    those who come late to the Work of God or to table.[1]

The insinuation here is that a lack of punctuality, which may of course be unavoidable at times, can cause upset to others and may even be a symptom of a certain disregard or disrespect for

those who have already made an effort to be there. In any case
the message is that in all situations where a group has been
upset by what one person does, or fails to do, some gesture of
apology can help. Indeed, this gesture can be thought of as a
kind of medicine because it helps to heal whatever hurts or
wounds may have been caused and to remove from the offend-
ing one an attitude which could have made him less acceptable
to all.

St Benedict, however, offers us another typical example of a
fault which can, when handled well, become a step upon the
journey to that promised land of peace. It is when someone
breaks or loses something and, in doing so, becomes the cause of
inconvenience to some others who may need that item, too.
Although such breaking or such losing may be no more than a
simple accident, the Rule requires that whosoever is responsible
for such a fault should

come at once of his own accord to *confess* his offence.[2]

Of course, that is, no doubt, what most of us would generally do,
although there could, we must admit, be times when the temptation to say nothing and to try 'to get away with it' can come into
our minds! However, to accept responsibility by making that
confession can become a step, not only on the road towards re-
integration with the group, but towards that integration of our
selves which is essential for our peace and for our human
growth.

* * *

There is also mention in the Rule of faults which are not, in
themselves, against the whole community, but just against one
other person of the group. The hurts, which faults like those can
cause, need to be healed, as well. The method which we choose,
however, may be different in every case and we, in fact, may
never use the one which is referred to in the Rule!

If any brother ... perceive that any senior, in whatever small
a degree, is displeased or angry with him, let him at once
without delay, cast himself on the ground and lie there, making reparation, until that displeasure is appeased, and he
bless him.[3]

Not each culture will suggest that every one who falls down in relating to another should fall down upon the ground as well! But we can often feel that, when we have offended someone, and not only those who are in some way 'senior' to ourselves, we should confess our fault and even, if we can, 'before the sun goes down'.[4] What is important in such situations, therefore, is to heal, as far as we are able, those whom we have hurt and, in so doing, to be open to receive into ourselves the healing which the blessing of their subsequent forgiveness can bestow.

Experience, however, can suggest another and a most important point. It is that when the Body, which is the community itself, is healed at that spot where it had been bruised, or even broken, then the Body as a whole, can benefit as well. When, for example, we resolve some problem in our own relationship with someone else the good that can result can often benefit not only us, but, maybe, many other people, too. The health which is restored to one small segment of the Body can, in other words, spread out, relieving tension in adjacent parts and then, perhaps, invigorating them as well. In such a way the Body as a whole is able to develop and, to quote a verse of Scripture, to 'upbuild itself in love'![5]

* * *

'Satisfaction' is a word which is, quite often, mentioned in the Rule. It is, in fact, included in its verbal form of 'making satisfaction' (or of 'making reparation') in that sentence which refers to the offender lying on the ground! What it suggests, however, is that frequently we have to settle for a period of time between our saying 'sorry' to a person whom we have offended and the reconciliation which is, ultimately, sought.

Indeed, the one whom we have hurt may often need a little time before that hurt is overcome and he or she is 'satisfied' and able to accept us once again. But, those who have offended may need time, as well. Although they may already have repented and apologised, they may discover that there is a certain worry or dis-ease within themselves which will not quickly go away. In fact, it can continue quite a while. But, when an inner calmness comes as they relate again to whomsoever they have hurt, they can suspect that the forgiving-blessing which the one who was offended gives, has actually worked!

There is one sentence in the Rule, however, which deserves a special mention here. It is the one which says that those who are responsible for some particular fault should:

make due satisfaction to God in the oratory.[6]

To God! That cannot mean that God himself requires a period of time before he can accept again the one who has offended him, for God cannot be hurt as human beings can! His nature is invulnerable and his love forever flows! Thus, what 'to make due satisfaction' to him must imply is that it would be good to let him ease the dis-ease in ourselves and, then, to fill us with his Spirit once again. In that way will the God, who is all-love, be fully satisfied!

* * *

One element in all this healing process which should be considered is the role of someone special who is not involved in the dynamics of the problem which upsets us at the time. An independent party can, indeed, be useful in some situations and, with his or her support and, maybe, some advice, we often can begin to cope much more successfully with some disturbed relationship or with whatever the annoying problem is. St Benedict respected such a need and even recommended that, when it arises, we should bring our worries to those people who

know how to cure their own wounds and the wounds of others without disclosing and publishing them.[7]

We will, of course, have to consider the importance of a Spiritual Father, or a Spiritual Mother, when we come to speak of 'listening' but such figures also merit mention in the context of that healing which is our consideration here. Such people can, both by their presence and, perhaps, by some effective word, convince us that, while others may need time before they can forgive us, God is always ready and can do so 'here and now'.

* * *

Wounds and healing; medicine and ointments, too! St Benedict, who uses all these words, does not say that a monastery is like a hospital but, in a sense, it is. It is a place where people who are less than perfect live and where, with the support of others[8] they can learn to cope with their own frailty and grow in spiritual health. It is a place, moreover, where they can receive 'the medicine of Holy Scripture'[9] and the stimulating ointment[10] of encouragement so that the life which they desire to have can flow within their spiritual veins. But, it is also an environment in which those very people who are being healed are able to discover that they can themselves become in many ways effective healers, too!

Each day, or rather twice a day, St Benedict would have his own disciples say 'the whole of the Lord's Prayer'.[11] The reason which he gives is:

> the removal of those thorns of scandal, or mutual offence, which are wont to arise in communities. For, being warned by the covenant which they make in that prayer, when they say 'Forgive us as we forgive', the brethren will cleanse their souls of such faults.[12]

There is a two-way movement indicated here. The first is our apology to God for all those 'thorns of scandal' for which we have been responsible; the second is our reaching out, forgivingly, to those whose 'thorns of scandal' have offended us. The two, however, go together, for the more that we ourselves receive that merciful forgiveness which comes to us from above, the more we will be able to transmit that same forgiveness to all those who, in their own lives, need it too.

And so, invigorated by the life which ultimately comes from God, we all can grow, not only into spiritual health, but also into Christ who now lives in that heavenly Jerusalem above[13] with him who is the Father of us all.

Patientia!

'Patience' is a very Benedictine word! We find it in a number of important places in the Rule but what is worth observing here is that it can suggest two almost contradictory things! So, for the benefit of those who have already found much wisdom in that ancient document, let us now spend a little time reflecting on this rather special word, and on the mystery it implies.

Let us begin by pondering a little Latin first!

The word for 'patience' in the Rule is *patientia* which does not sound too different from the English form we know. But *patientia* would have reminded those who knew the Rule in Latin of another Latin word, the verb 'to suffer', which is *patior* or, in the perfect, *passus sum*. So *patientia* would have suggested, much more strongly than its English counterpart can do today, an element of suffering in our lives. To say that we were patient, therefore, would have meant that we were the recipients of some misfortune or of some injustice which was done. In other words it would have signified that we were then receiving, passively, some kind of passion in our lives!

However, among Christians, *patientia* was understood within the context of the total Christian mystery and, so, it could imply, not only suffering, but hope! St Peter, for example, writing in the early days of Christianity, could say to those who found the going hard:

> Rejoice in as far as you share Christ's sufferings (*passiones*) that you may also rejoice and be glad when his glory is revealed.[1]

The *passiones* of those early Christians were, he knew, in some way, taken up and joined to those of Christ himself. But, since the *passio* (or sufferings) of Christ led to an everlasting life, so, too, St Peter here reminds his readers, can their own! As for St Benedict, he also was convinced that all the sufferings which he himself envisaged as he wrote his Rule would lead those who accepted them with patience to that satisfying culmination, too.

The *passiones* which St Benedict envisaged were, however, not of that kind which would normally involve a violent death. They were the ordinary trials which most of us experience as we respond to people and to situations every day. But in their own way, as St Benedict suggests, such *passiones* can be crucifying, too! What he desires to emphasise, however, is that, just as Lent gives way to Easter,[2] so these sufferings can lead those who accept them patiently to everlasting life. That was the reason why in different places he was able to refer to, and indeed exude, anticipated joy.[3]

* * *

One of the places where we meet this word is in that chapter which supplies the tools or instruments for living well. There, among the others in the Garden Shed, the following is found:

to bear patiently the wrongs done to oneself.[4]

That was a counsel of perfection which St Benedict himself had learnt and which he recommends to all who feel that they have been in some way injured by another. Many would, of course, declare that in such circumstances people should not be so passive but, instead, assertive and demanding of their 'rights'. But, while that counsel can at times be good, at other times, perhaps, there often is a better and a wiser way and it is that which needs some advertising now!

Let me begin by mentioning that story from the *Dialogues* which tells us how St Benedict behaved when persecuted by a jealous priest. Instead of being angry and, perhaps, vindictive in return, St Benedict, the story goes, decided to move quietly away. That was, it could be argued, to admit defeat and in a sense it was. But, on the other hand, in bearing patiently the wrong done to himself, he kept his inner peace and, in his going to another place, he found a whole new life which he might never have discovered had he stayed. Indeed, it was the treachery of that same priest which made it possible for him to start that monastery on Monte Cassino which was later to become so famous and from which his name and influence, in later centuries, would spread. It is a salutary thought that if St Benedict had not accepted patiently the wrong done to himself, the glory which he now enjoys might never have been his![5]

The same is true of Christ. He, too, accepted patiently the sufferings which came his way and, therefore, found that new existence which is now forever his. St Gregory, who intimates that in this way he was the model for St Benedict himself, suggests that he can be the same for all of Benedict's disciples, too.

* * *

Another place where we can find a reference to patience in the Rule is, as we might expect, within the famous chapter on the sick. However, there the emphasis may take us by surprise. It does not say that those who are unwell ought to be patient (though of course they should) but that all those who care for them should have this sympathetic gift! The sick, St Benedict declares:

should be borne with patiently.[6]

That is a statement which suggests that, maybe, sometimes they were not! Indeed the sick can be demanding, as all those who minister to them know, and it is sometimes easy to become impatient with them, too! St Benedict, however, who would always want such ministers to have whatever help they need, would also want them to appreciate the fact that, through accepting patiently whatever inroads on their time and energy are made, they too are able to receive the promise and, indeed, the first instalments of a very great reward.[7]

But let us ponder this idea of *patientia* a little more. Let us admit that, if the person in the bed is called a patient (since that person suffers) those who care for people in that state deserve, at times, to be described as patients, too! The one in bed may suffer from some physical disease but those who care for those who are unwell may suffer sometimes from a dis-ease of another kind! Thus, both the patient in the bed and those who minister are both participating in that mystery of suffering which, as we all know, is infiltrating everywhere! But such a universal *passio*, according to St Benedict and Christian teaching as a whole, is but the entrance to another life because it finds its focus and its meaning in the *passio* of the now-risen Christ!

* * *

There is another sentence in the Rule which makes a reference to patience. It is found in chapter 72 and it declares:

> let them bear with the greatest patience one another's infirmities whether of body or character.[8]

It is a sentence which is often quoted, so, it merits special mention, here.

Infirmities! The reference in this case is not just to those infirmities which were suggested in the chapter on the sick, but also to those many other ones which come to light when personalities of different kinds are living in one place. Indeed, in reading through the Rule, and in between the lines, one can imagine many people in St Benedict's community who could have been considered as 'infirm'! Were there not those who used to come, on some occasions, late to Office or to meals and one begins to wonder if there were not some who never could arrive on time for anything at all? Could there not also have been some in his community who had a special charism for losing or misplacing (or just breaking) things which others would require? Indeed, there was a famous notice in one monastery which mournfully proclaimed 'we used to have two dozen mugs and now there's only one!' And, then, there were the murmurers who constantly complained! However, while St Benedict had, certainly, a lot of less-than-perfect people on his list, the point that he is making here is that one needs not only patience, but the greatest patience if one is to live with such a tantalising crowd!

And yet this patience which we need with others often has to be with our own sometimes-disappointing selves, as well! That is a thought which is, in fact, included in the very sentence I have quoted from the Rule, although to see it clearly we will have to go back to the Latin text. There, we can find a word, an adjective, which had a double sense! It could have meant that what it qualifies (in this case the infirmities) are found by people either in each other or, reflexively, within themselves. Our sentence, therefore, can be re-translated thus:

> Let them bear with the greatest patience the infirmities of one another *and those of themselves*, whether of body or of character.[9]

Those of ourselves! There is no need to list the ways in which we can let both ourselves and others down. But it may be of value to point out again that there is also something stable in us too. It is that deepest part of our own being which is rooted in the one who made us and who is stability itself. And so we can be patient, even very patient, with our limitations and defects and know that God, who can turn disappointment into hope, can grow through what we actually are.

Part Four

Awareness

When Benedict was standing just above the town of Subiaco he could see, in front of him, the mountain slopes descending to the valley of the Aniane below. Then, when he raised his eyes again, there was the sky, that sky which can, at times, be spotted with some light and scattered clouds. It was a peaceful vista and it must have been inspiring, too, for there, as we are told, he stayed.

Later, when he travelled south and settled on the summit of Monte Cassino, he beheld another view. It was the fertile plain which stretched out far below him with a range of other mountains and their peaks beyond. It, too, must have impressed him as he gazed at it each day.

Then, much later in his life, when he was writing what was to become his very famous Rule he opted to include a statement which, perhaps, recalled such awe-inspiring moments. It was:
    God is present everywhere.[1]
But Benedict did not elaborate on that particular thought for he was merely using it to introduce another which he wanted at that place to emphasise. However, when we isolate these introductory words, we cannot help but link them with those moments when he gazed at nature and allowed its beauty and its majesty to seep into his thirsty and receptive soul!

But all of us have had, to some degree, enriching moments of that kind. I can, myself, remember sitting on a rocky mountainside and gazing at the blueness of a bay below where specks of white, some foam, some yachts, lay floating on the sea. I can remember standing on a cliff which seemed to drop without a hesitation towards the water far below, with a half a dozen seagulls flying halfway down. I have sat on a hillside, too, and gazed at radiating valleys which a ruined fortress just behind me still seemed to control. And I remember, many many years ago, an afternoon when gently-flowing river-water and the quiet movement of some ducks, together with the sunshine, forced themselves so well into my mind that I could spend a long time afterwards reflecting on the scene. God was in all those situations, too!

Sometimes, when a new retreatant comes, I think of moments such as those. If, for example, he or she appears a little anxious (lest some precious time be lost!) and if I find myself being asked 'what should I do?' or 'how should I begin?' those memories can come to my assistance and I answer: 'Why not go out for a while and celebrate the sacrament of place?' 'Why not go out and see the avenues, the lakes, the trees?' 'Why not go out and listen to the singing of the birds?' 'Why not go out and smell the flowers, the grass, the very air itself?' God is in all of them. And, when they find him in those many things, he has himself a way of telling them what he wants them to do!

* * *

St Benedict was also conscious of a sacred presence in the people whom he knew. The evidence for that is, ultimately, in the way that he could say that Christ was in them all.[2] But let us see if we can find this presence for ourselves!

One of the 'tools' for this, which we can take from his collection, is:

to honour all.[3]

It is, of course, an adaptation of the old commandment, 'honour your father and your mother', and St Benedict, presumably, considered that it was a form more suitable for those who had, in fact, left home! The people to whom he and his disciples would have had to show both honour and respect would have been those who came to meet them, for some purpose, in their prayerful solitude. But now the Rule is offering this 'tool' to us to use within the context of our own, quite frequently more complicated, lives. It is suggesting that, instead of using people for our own advantage, which we can so easily do, we should discover how to see and reverence the goodness which is in them and which seeks an opportunity to grow!

This may require, at times, a little effort on our part. Some people may not seem at first to be particularly good but, with the help of God, we can begin to see and to admire what frequently so many others miss. A recent Benedictine writer, Bishop Gerry, put it well when he wrote in a recent book:

> Look up on a clear night and what do you see? A random scattering of stars. A navigator can pick out a pattern that could enable him to steer a ship. Look at an X-ray and what do you see? A technician can identify a broken bone. We see what we are trained to see! And much depends on what we are looking for. The pure in heart look for the good in others. And when we see the good in others we are catching a glimpse of God himself.[4]

Then, nourished by our recognition of their Godness, Godness in those very people may discover that it has its opportunity to grow!

Is that what is implied by saying 'Christ is in the people whom we meet?' It surely is for Christ is God-made-visible and in a story we are told how Benedict himself perceived that presence in an unexpected guest. It was a priest who, when he was about to sit down and enjoy his Easter dinner, had an inspiration to go out and seek the hermit who was living in the hills and, then, to share all that he had with him, 'For this is Easter Day' he said, by way of explanation when he reached the isolated cave, to which the Man of God replied:

> I know it is Easter Day because I have been granted to see thee![5]

Does that not indicate that there can be an incarnated and a beneficial presence in the people who in different ways come into our own lives?

* * *

Some years ago I asked a group of visitors, 'what exactly do you think are the essential qualities of Benedictine life?' To my surprise they all stressed in their answer its 'respect for matter' and 'the reverence which it can have for even ordinary things'. It was not, I admit, the kind of answer that I had expected at the time but I could not help feeling that they, probably, were touching an important, if perhaps a secondary, point. Now, on reflection, I am sure, not only that this quality is most important, but that 'secondary' does not mean that it does not flow from the very centre of the life itself. However, we, perhaps, should think about this quality a little more.

Let me begin by saying that a lot of Benedictine monasteries have workshops and that some communities are even noted for some special form of art activity, as well. For example, there are some where metal-work is done and others where some members are involved in pottery or in some other art or craft. Then, going back to medieval days there were quite obviously many artists who, with loving care, produced the carvings and the stain-glass windows which can still be seen and so admired today. And, going even further back, we can discover in the Rule itself a chapter which is totally devoted to

the craftsmen of the monastery.[6]

That would suggest that working with material things is, certainly, as those few visitors of mine declared, a fairly vital and important part of Benedictine life.

But let us note again a sentence in the Rule. It says when speaking of the Cellarer:

let him look upon all the utensils of the monastery and its whole property as upon the sacred vessels of the altar.[7]

Utensils! Property! This would include, not only implements and other things belonging to the 'craftsmen', but all kinds of things from pots and pans to ordinary furniture which everybody used. The purpose of this exhortation in the Rule was, probably, to urge that all those things should be respected and maintained in good condition for the use of those who needed them each day. But this expression of St Benedict seems to imply much more. That he could say that all those ordinary things possess a sacred quality suggests, not only that he thought of them as dedicated to the Lord (which in a monastery would be the case), but that they somehow manifested something of God's hidden presence to him, too!

'Like sacred vessels of the altar!' Let us ponder this comparison
a little more. It seems to say that, while those ordinary things
may manifest some attribute of the divinity, they need our help
if they are to reveal the very essence of his life. For example,
when we use them in a truly human way they can reveal, not
just the power or wisdom or the beauty of their Maker[8] but the
love which he is offering to everyone, as well. Within the liturgy
of life the humblest article can play a valuable part in both re-
vealing and communicating what is, in itself, divine!

Responsive Listening

'To listen', as we have already noted, is a verb which in the Latin language is related to the one which we translate as 'to obey'. 'To listen' to another person, therefore, should imply that we are ready 'to obey' that other person, too. Of course this does not always happen, as we know. To say the least, we frequently can be much less responsive to another person than that other person wants. But, on the other hand, if we are listening to that person 'with the heart', our inclination 'to obey' that person will most certainly increase. Indeed, in such a situation we can be disposed to do, not only what that other person actually asks, but frequently much more!

Let us consider these dynamics in the context of our own relationship with God. He speaks to us (admittedly in different ways). We hear, (again in different ways and frequently not even in a way which tells us that he is the one who speaks). However, since his Word is ultimately spoken to the heart, when we are really listening we will surely want to do what he in fact desires, whatever that may be. Of course, a lot of other voices may distract us but his Word has its own way of touching our own deeper selves and, when that happens, we can sometimes even find ourselves responding with that unrestrained 'obedience without delay!'[1] which is envisaged in the Rule. When that occurs, or rather when we notice that it has occurred, we can be fairly sure that we were, at that very moment, being animated by the Spirit which the God, who is all-love, had put into our hearts.

* * *

God speaks to us in many ways and, frequently, it is through people who, in some way, influence our lives.

When we were small it was, most probably, through parents that God told us what to do. Then, as we grew, it may have been through teachers, friends or even chance acquaintances that he revealed to us the wisdom which we needed at the time. And, later, other people had, no doubt, their influence, as well.

In this we are to some extent like streams which, as they travel, are increased by other streams which flow down from a mountainside until they grow into a strong and noble river which eventually flows into the vastness of the sea. Of course, this metaphor is limited because our stream must feed the streams of others just as much as it needs to be fed by theirs! However, it does illustrate how much the progress of each individual depends on quite a hinterland of influence if he or she is to develop and grow well.

At times, this stream which represents ourselves cannot afford to race along without a thought nor to meander, as it were, without a care. When we come up against some problem and begin to realise that some decision must be made, we need to stop (as if to form a lake!) and to accept the contributions which (like numerous in-flowing streams!) those who are close to us can make. Enlightened, then, by what such people say, we should be better able to perceive what we should do and how we should proceed. Indeed, the Rule itself envisages this method of procedure when it says:

> do all things with counsel and thy deeds shall not bring thee repentance.[2]

Did St Benedict, who chose this verse from Sirach,[3] know of certain people who, had they accepted some advice, would not have made a mess of their own lives? Perhaps he did and, maybe, we know some such people, too! In any case, it is by seeking and by using all the wisdom we can glean (a wisdom which, of course, comes ultimately from above[4]) that we can grow into that strong and noble river which keeps moving on successfully towards the everlasting sea!

* * *

There is one type of person through whom God speaks to us in a very special way. It the 'spiritual father', or the 'abbot', who is able to assist us on the road which leads to peace. The 'spiritual mother' or the 'abbess' is, of course the female counterpart.

It should, perhaps, be noted here that in the early Church all those who were about to be baptised would have been guided by a kind of 'Abba-figure' as they learnt to live as Christian people should. Today the Rite of Baptism for Adults still presumes, not only the existence of such sponsors, but their vital contribution to the lives of those who are about to be baptised. The Rule takes this a further step and emphasises that the monk should have an Abba-person too. However, what it seems to say to non-monastic readers is that, maybe, they should also think about the value of acquiring some such comparable person for themselves if they desire to let that life which they received through Baptism develop and grow strong.

Dependence on an Abba-figure can, however, vary quite a lot.

A monk would normally look to his 'abbot' for a lot of guidance at the start of his monastic life but, later on, he would, no doubt, be able to apply the basic principles of that life by himself. If, later still, and after many years of living in community, he were to graduate to live a hermit's life (as is at least envisaged by the Rule[5]) his contact with his abbot would become inevitably less. In spite of that, however, some such Abba-figure would continue as a guiding and supportive person whom he could consult at certain moments and as somebody to whom he could, with confidence, reveal his struggles and his failings and, perhaps, his falls!

The pattern for non-monastic Christians who have chosen some kind of an Abba-figure would most probably be much the same.

In any case what is important for such guidance to be fruitful is great openness of soul! The Rule itself tells the disciple to
> confess and conceal not from his abbot any evil thoughts that
> enter his heart and any secret sins that he has committed.[6]

This, it goes on to explain, ought to be done because the Abbot (and such spiritual fathers)
> know how to cure their own wounds and the wounds of others without disclosing or publishing them.[7]

The purpose of such openness is, therefore, let us note, not just for guidance only, but for spiritual healing, too!

What we are speaking about here is fairly close to what we call the Sacrament of Confession or, at least, to how in recent centuries that Sacrament has frequently been used. But there are certain differences, too! The Sacrament was first of all designed for those who had committed one of those offences which exclude the sinner from the life of the community itself (that is the Church) and so, in it, it has to be the bishop or a delegated priest (who represents the whole community) who reconciles the one who has confessed. What we are now considering, however, are those venial sins, especially those which are known to no one but ourselves and which, although there is no obligation to confess them in the Sacrament, can hinder both our own growth and our unity with others too. Do we not need some trusted person, therefore, who will listen to us when we need to speak about the struggles and the imperfections in ourselves? Do we not need some Abba-person who is able to assure us that God loves us all the time and that, in spite of everything, all can and will be well? When somebody does that for us, whoever it may be, that moment surely is, to use the word in a wider sense, a sacramental moment too. Through it, God, who is able to accept us as we are, gives us the grace of his own Spirit to become what he himself desires!

* * *

God also speaks to us through people from the past!

We have already noted how St Benedict desired his followers to spend some time each day at 'lectio divina' but, within the context of this chapter, something more needs to be said. It is that as we do our 'lectio divina' we can hear the words of those inspired religious teachers who, in different ways, made such a vital contribution to the lives of people in the past. A few, like Jeremiah and Isaiah, Matthew, Paul, and John, we know by name but there were many others, like the writers of the psalms, who stayed anonymous and, in the Rule St Benedict quite frequently refers to them with the generic title of 'the prophet'. This implies that, as he pondered what they said, he got the inspiration for his own life which he needed at the time. But what he is suggesting is that we, in being open to their words, may find a comparable inspiration, too!

The Scriptures are the words of people but they always have been understood to be in some mysterious way the Word of God, as well. Through all the many things which all the very different human authors say, a long tradition echoes the conviction that to those-who-have-the-ears-to-hear, it is the Lord himself who speaks. St Benedict acknowledged this tradition for, at times, instead of saying 'as the prophet said', he says that such-and-such a psalm-verse, or whatever he is quoting, is addressed to us by 'God' or by 'the Lord'. Of course, in many cases and especially when what is said is obviously less than perfect, what we read will have to be associated with some other passage if we are to recognise in it the voice that is divine! But with a little effort and a prayerful spirit that instructive voice which speaks so lovingly can always be discerned.

* * *

At this point let us speak of silence!

St Benedict devoted one whole chapter to it in his Rule and in a number of the others he referred to it as well. His emphasis, however, is, perhaps, a little disappointing for he does not actually give the ultimate and fully satisfying reason for its cultivation in our lives. Yet there is little doubt that silence was for him what it was to become for many others: the relaxing atmosphere in which what God is saying to us can be heard.

However, human nature and its growth demand that talk, and quite a lot of it at times, be often activated too! We need to talk if, for example, we require some guidance or advice from someone else or if we are to answer those who seek the same from us. Indeed, we need to talk if we are going to build up those interpersonal relationships which are important for our lives! It is not too surprising, then, to find that in the Rule, which presupposes that there are occasions when we ought to speak, the thrust is, not to stop all speech, but just to prune its use! Thus, in the 'Garden Shed' collection of advice we are exhorted 'not to love

much speaking',[8] while the chapter 'On Observing Lent' encour-
ages the reader 'to stint himself of ... talk and jesting'![9] It would
seem that what St Benedict desired was to encourage his disciples to create an atmosphere in which they could be more attentive to the Word which comes from God himself – and to the
whisperings of his Spirit in their lives.

Before we search the Rule for further comments on the value of
this silence, let us note that for St Benedict there is a kind of talk
which can do damage not just to the hearers, but to those who
speak, as well. The Rule itself contains a reference to one (a
monk, of course!),

> who spends his time in idleness and gossip ... so that he not
> only does himself harm but also disturbs others.[10]

This idea that gossiping can harm the gossiper may take us by
surprise but, on reflection, we can see that it is true! Indeed, the
gossip, which may only for a while disturb another, is more likely
to remain within the speaker's mind and there, of course, it can
begin to circulate and, then, to influence the way that he or she
behaves. There is, moreover, something of a downward spiral
indicated here because, instead of being open to (or vacant for)
the edifying Scriptures, those who peddle gossip can be 'open
to' not only idleness, but further gossip, too.[11]

Perhaps, however, it is just because a lot of chat, and not a little
gossip, are so much a part of human life, that on the Ladder of
Humility there is no reference to silence until many steps have
been already climbed. This seems to indicate that Benedict himself,
who took this Ladder passage from another,[12] felt that silence-
with-contentment only comes with age when many things in life
have been resolved. Indeed, the silence which he advocates is
one which can suggest a certain wisdom[13] and, as everybody
knows, that is a gift which was especially associated with the
old! However, just as shrubs which will, in time, produce abun-
dant fruit require some pruning at an early stage so, too, do people if they are to have at least a chance of growing wise! Thus, in
another chapter of his Rule,[14] St.Benedict tells all his followers
that even what they might consider to be good and edyfying
conversation should, at times, give way to silence which they,
consequently, can consider to be good and even edifying too!

The silence which we need, however, is not just from talk but also from the noise of many thoughts. A time must, therefore, come when we should be content, not only not to speak, but just, as one would say today, to be. Indeed, I sometimes say to a retreatant, who does not appear to have a problem which deserves to be discussed: 'relax, stop thinking', and I sometimes add 'and do not even think of God!' That can cause some surprise. But just as there can come a time when thoughts can stop an ordinary human friendship from developing as it should so, too, can they impede the growth of our relationship with God! And so, just be and let him be, and true communication will inevitably, at a deep and fruitful level, happen, too.

* * *

What next?

A lot of people are discovering the value of at least a period of 'silent time' each day. Some are, moreover, finding for themselves how much this kind of period can be enriched by knowing something of the old, contemplative tradition of the Church and that for them is often wonderful, indeed. But, while a pattern of quiet prayer will certainly enable them to have a better-balanced life, it may, at times, lead them to wonder: 'is that all or is there something else which I should do?'

St Benedict does not provide an answer. He does not suggest that there is anything which we should do apart from what he has already said. Indeed, he often seems to think that all we need to do is to continue as we are, although we must admit, of course, that with a deeper form of prayer we may be able to improve our lectio and, maybe, to be more discerning in the area of work. However, what St Benedict accepts is that there are some ways in which we can facilitate the transformation of our very lives which God, and our own deeper selves, desire. They are referred to in the chapter on that famous Ladder of Humility which we must now examine briefly here.

But first, a word about the nature of the journey which the climbing of this Ladder of Humility implies. It is, according to St Benedict, a journey into love. You will recall how he began his

Spiritual Charter by referring to the great commandments and how, later, he concluded with the promise that we can attain that perfect love which is not limited by fear.

> When all these degrees of humility have been climbed the monk will come to that perfect love of God which casts out all fear.[15]

That 'all', of course, does not include that 'reverential love', 'respect' or even 'awe', which, far from hindering our love, protects it, and enables it to grow. Such 'fear' will never cease. But every kind which can impede us on our journey into God and, therefore, into unity with those whom he is calling, too, is meant to disappear!

* * *

This 'journey into love' is likened by St Benedict (as we have noted) to the climbing of a Ladder but this is a Ladder which, as he explains,[16] can only be ascended by a climber who is also, at the same time, 'going down'! This is, of course, a paradoxical procedure and the exhortation to the one who wants to reach the top to let go of his own desires describes it fairly well! To him St Benedict himself says:

> Turn aside from your own will.[17]

Of course, he means that 'will' which springs from our not-yet-redeemed-and-rooted-selves and not those deeper yearnings which come from our fundamental and essential selves. What he is really saying, therefore, is that, if we notice a dichotomy within ourselves, we should be ready to ignore all those desires which do not seem to come from God (and which can, therefore, lead us into situations which we, later, would regret). He wants us to be free to follow those more noble yearnings which, we can presume, God has himself inspired.

The first step on the Ladder, therefore, is to grow aware of God's all-seeing presence and to learn how to respond to his demands. The second step repeats the exhortation not to follow the desires which come from our (unanchored) selves but it suggests a new dimension, too. It is that, as we do what God seems to desire, we are reflecting in some way the life of Christ himself! The third step on the ladder brings us further and proposes that in every situation we should 'imitate the Lord' in his obedience to God.

However, it reminds us that that normative obedience, which leads of course to everlasting life, was at the same time even 'unto death'! Such is the paradox of which the Ladder speaks.

However, it is when St Benedict is speaking of the fourth step on the Ladder of Humility that he presents us with what is, perhaps, his most demanding challenge. He refers to moments when we meet 'with difficulties and contradictions and even injustice' in our lives and says that, in such situations, we should:

> with a quiet mind hold fast to patience and enduring neither tire nor run away.[18]

It should be noted that he is not here referring to those situations which demand that we address some problem in an active (although peaceful) way, although it could be said that there, as well, some perservering patience would not go amiss. What he is saying is that there are moments when a calm and very trusting patience by itself (and patience is a very Benedictine word!) is all that we require! God will himself, in time, show us what we should do!

A wise old monk who taught me once said that this step upon the Ladder of Humility was Benedict's Beecher's Brook! For those who are not so familiar with the racing world, he was referring to that complicated jump at Aintree which is both a hedge and, then, a rising slope! How my mentor got his information I was never told but, certainly, that jump brings down a good percentage of the horses every year. Of course, it may not be completely fair to think of life in terms of the Grand National but, if the different steps upon this Ladder have for us an element of challenge, it could well be argued that the fourth is the most difficult of all. However, we have many guides, including Paul whom Benedict quotes twice in this important passage. But his over-riding guide, of course, was Christ himself, who always trusted in his Father's powerful love and knew that in doing so he would win the promised prize!

* * *

There are twelve steps on this Ladder of Humility. The first four (plus some others) have already been referred to in this chapter and another few will be considered in the next. The 12th, and final step, however, though it paints a somewhat unattractive picture of how those who reach the top appear could be, if only indirectly, noted here.

First let me focus on the author's own conclusion to this chapter on Humility (and to his Spiritual Charter as a whole). In it we find a most important sentence which puts both the twelfth and all the other steps, as well, into a new perspective and, in doing so, gives them a meaning and a value which, in turn, makes them more possible to climb. It is that what each one of them implies

the Lord (will) deign to show forth by the power of his Spirit in his workman.[19]

Thus, while Benedict continues to accept that we must always, like a workman, do our best (in pulling weeds or climbing steps!) he stresses that, when all is done, we will be able to appreciate the fact that it was God himself who had been working in us all the time. The top step of this ladder indicates that God is also able to reveal himself through everything we do.

This twelfth step tells us that a monk:

should not only be humble of heart, but should also in his behaviour always manifest his humility to those who look upon him.

Maybe the description which St Benedict goes on to give us here does not have much appeal to many in this day and age. Indeed, it might be argued that, if he had not felt so obliged to keep intact an older and an honoured text, he might have offered us a more attractive one! But, having said that, we have to admit that once again we find the basic paradox: the ladder is ascended only by those who are willing to descend! Thus, it is only when we know that we are totally unworthy of God's love that his love will be able to express itself completely through our lives!

* * *

When speaking of responding to the love of God in Benedictine terms one must include some mention of Scholastica. She was, according to St Gregory, the sister of St Benedict and every year, he tells us,[20] they would meet. However, on what was to be their final meeting, something unexpected happened which must be related here.

When evening came and it was getting late, Scholastica looked at her brother and requested that he would not leave so that they could continue talking and, of course, enjoy the peace which their own spiritual sharing would provide. However, Benedict who was prepared to go replied: 'Nay, sister, do not ask for that for I may not remain outside my monastery!' Scholastica then bowed her head. She prayed and suddenly a storm arose, a storm which was so great that Benedict, in spite of his intentions, had no option but to stay. Scholastica's request was answered after all!

The story is a good one but the comment of St Gregory needs to be noted, too. It is that we should not be too surprised that God was pleased to answer the petition of Scholastica and, thereby, overrule the plan of Benedict himself. The reason which he gives is that she 'had the greater love'. What does that mean? Perhaps, it is that, while she knew that rules can be important guides she knew, as well, that they must bow to those desires which God himself inspires! Indeed, a human rule, however great, can only do so much. Love, which both comes from God and yearns for him, is always the essential element of life.

One cannot help but wonder if a free, spontaneous response to God, which can be thought of as personified by St Scholastica, is feminine in itself! The fact is that while she, no doubt, had her own rule of life, for she was also 'dedicated to the service of the Lord', her brother, who was so intent on keeping his, discovered that, on this occasion, there was something he could learn from her. Perhaps, as we might say today, it was to let the feminine within himself develop so that he could have the sensitivity to hear what God was really saying in a situation and, of course, the courage to respond. Perhaps, we all must do the same! Indeed, according to the Scriptures, the community, which is the Church itself, is feminine in its relationship to God! It is the bride which listens and which, then, responds with love to Christ, who is its ever-present, ever-loving Lord.

Contentment

There is a chapter in the Rule about receiving pilgrim monks. It says, as we would probably expect, that they are to be welcomed but it also manifests an openness which may, perhaps, take us a little by surprise. It states that, if the pilgrim monk who is accepted is content with what he finds and if he has no obligation to return to any other monastery, he may be even urged to stay!

In those days, as to some extent in ours, there were those 'unconnected' monks or people who were living a religious way of life but on their own and, so, without the help which a community (and some well-chosen guide) could give.[1] It is, moreover, not unlikely that a number would have come from time to time to centres such as those for which St Benedict composed his Rule. But, if they did and if it was discovered that they were 'content with the customs of the place',[2] the abbot of the monastery in which they were might ask, or even urge, them to remain. It would, he might suggest, be easier for them to grow in their own spiritual life if they had some more regular support! However, what concerns us here is that contentment which is necessary for their rooting and, by implication, for their spiritual growth, as well.

* * *

This is, perhaps, the moment to consider one more step upon the famous Ladder of Humility. It is a step which may at first seem unappealing but it does contain the word which is our subject for reflection here. It says:

> the sixth degree (step) of humility is that a monk be content with the meanest and worst of everything, and esteem himself, in regard to the work that is given him, as a bad and unworthy workman![3]

This ideal which St Benedict has taken from his major source, should not, however, be interpreted as meaning that the monk, or anybody else, ought to desire the 'worst of everything' as if that was a virtue in itself. Nor does it mean that we ought to develop in ourselves a low and self-destructive self-esteem! Indeed, St Benedict, who wanted his communities to be 'administered by prudent people in a prudent manner'[4] could not have intended such a thing. It is more likely, therefore, that he meant that those who keep their inner peace, despite not having the facilities which they require or even the accomplishments which they would like, possess in their contentment something which is more important and, indeed, much more to be desired.

However, let us also call to mind a sentence which we have already seen. It is the theological conclusion to the chapter on Humility which says that

> this the Lord will deign to show forth by the power of his Spirit in his workman.[5]

This, of course, refers to all the graces which the twelve steps on the Ladder had implied. However, in the context of the sixth step we can come to one particular conclusion. It is that our own contentment, when it comes, is not fruit of what we do, or even of our attitudes. It is the work of God's own Spirit in our lives.

Contentment, therefore, is a sign that those who really have it, have within themselves the very presence of that satisfying Spirit, too!

* * *

There is one final step which does demand some mention here. It is the rather awesome number seven which suggests a breaking through into a new stage of awareness in our lives. It is a step, moreover, from which all the very ordinary ones which follow (and which we in fact have seen) can be regarded and accepted with an ease not previously known. But, for the moment, let us contemplate this seventh step and ponder what is said about it in the text.

It says that he who has attained this rung will:

> not only in his speech declare himself lower and of less account than all others, but should in his inmost heart believe it.[6]

Such a declaration does not use the word *content*. When we have pondered what it means, however, we no doubt will realise that only those who are, in fact, content will have the power to balance on this difficult, if liberating, rung. But, meanwhile, maybe we could note the verses from the psalms which, in the text, are added to the declaration I have quoted here. They can facilitate our understanding of the way that that rung can be reached.

Before we look at them, however, let us note that it is most unlikely that St Benedict was asking his disciples in the first part of this text to look at one another and to gauge their own development by what their neighbours seem to be. He, certainly, did not want any monk or any follower of his to boast, with false humility, that he or she was less important or of less account than anybody else. It is more likely, therefore, that, in this text which he borrowed from his major source, he only wanted to convince the ones who did that just believing it was really quite enough! We smile, perhaps, that such a comment could have been required at all. But, while it does contain a fact which all of us can fairly easily accept, we know that 'to believe it in the heart' (and with contentment, too!) is much more difficult and many may consider it to be impossible as well! Indeed, St Benedict would not completely disagree. He knew that this can only happen with the grace of God and as a consequence of all that disillusionment about one's own importance which life teaches us in time.

However, let us here examine some of those quotations from the psalms which have been added to the text and which appear to illustrate the devastating and transforming stages of our lives. One, for example, seems to speak about a person who was doing all he should and doing it quite well. '*I have been lifted up*' he says. But, then, life seems to have, in some way, undermined a certain self-reliance which was previously his and, if he had in fact felt *lifted up*, he now feels that he is not so important or so central to the universe, at all! He has been *humbled* and, perhaps, *confounded*, too! However, life goes on and, in the next psalm which is quoted, he begins to settle and discover that what may have been a difficult or shattering experience had actually helped him to perceive the meaning and the value of his life as he had never done before. He, therefore, with an unexpected gratitude, can turn again to God and say that: 'It is good that you have humbled me'. A new and deeper level of contentment has, apparently, been found!

The person who has reached this seventh step is, therefore, one who has become aware, from personal experience, that all things, even life itself, come as a gift from God! But such a person knows as well, that, even when life feels completely empty, God is always present and, moreover, that he is a loving Father, too. The new contentment which that person finds is, consequently, one of satisfying, if not always glowing, peace. It is a gift which makes it possible for those who have it to make further progress into God.[7] It is a gift, however, which we can receive through quietly accepting what is in itself a self-annihilating truth: that is, that in the depths of our own being, we already, at this very moment, live and move in him![8]

* * *

Contentment is related to the verb *contain*. But this verb can be used, as we have seen, in two completely different ways. For example, we can say that something is *containing* something else or that it is itself *contained*. Thus, to apply this to the case which we have been considering, we can declare that we are both containing and contained. To spell this out: each one of us contains the Spirit of the living God while, on the other hand, we are contained in his enfolding Spirit, too! God is, in other words, both in and all around us and it is in these two complementary ways that he allows us to experience from time to time that gift of deep contentment in which we, who do not try to do so, can expand!

Part Five

Back to the Beginning!

The Prologue to the Rule of Benedict is a classic In itself. It is, moreover, that part of the total document which is the most attractive for the non-monastic reader of today. Of course, it has been influenced, and to a very large degree, by that monastic rule[1] to which I have quite frequently referred. But, through that more immediate source, it echoes even older thoughts which may have come from some baptismal homily of the very early Church. That would, to some extent, explain why it can have such value for so many people who are simply looking for some extra guidance in their spiritual lives. I have decided, therefore, to conclude this introduction to the mind of Benedict by reproducing here the full text of the Prologue with some (hopefully not-too-distracting) comments of my own!

But let me, first of all, make one brief introductory remark. It is that, if the structure of the Prologue is not easy to define, there are some themes which both appear and reappear. They are, moreover, themes which we, who have already read a lot of what the Rule itself contains, will quickly recognise. Awareness, listening, absolute commitment, service of each other and the need for grace if we are to continue well are some and to that list we could add hope or expectation of eternal life. In fact this sequence, with small alterations, seems to be repeated three times in the text itself and so I have decided for convenience to employ this somewhat arbitrary analysis and to divide this chapter into three main sections, too.

* * *

Harken, my son, to the precepts of the Master and incline the ear of your heart. Freely accept and faithfully fulfil the instructions of a loving father, that by the labour of obedience you may return to him from whom you have strayed by the sloth of disobedience.

'A loving Father'! One could say, and many have, that this refers to Benedict himself. He is the father (and the master) who is speaking to us as we read the Rule just as he was for those for whom it was composed. But, on the other hand, we could say that the term refers to God. Is it not he from whom we all have strayed? Indeed, St Benedict, in contrast to his source,[2] makes this interpretation the more likely of the two.

One question here, however, comes to mind. It is, did he who spoke of God as 'loving Father' think of him as 'loving Mother' too? This is, of course, a question which St Benedict himself would, probably, have thought a little strange. However, it deserves at least a mention here for there are readers of the Rule today who claim that it possesses properties which are, if not maternal, certainly quite feminine! They say, to give a very general example, that it can facilitate the growth of sympathetic and assisting people rather than of macho and competing ones! If there is any truth in that, and I suspect there is, we must agree that Benedict himself, and so the God who guided him, had qualities or attributes which we, at least, can recognise as feminine, if not maternal, too!

However, whether feminine in ways or not, the God of Benedict bestowed on him a gift of wisdom which was very practical, indeed. The reader of this book may have already come to that conclusion since a number of the sentences which I have quoted here, seem to imply that fact. However, let us also note how in the Prologue Benedict presents himself in words which are themselves suggestive of a sage. Thus, copying the author of the Book of Proverbs who had written: 'Listen, to your father's instruction, do not reject your mother's teaching',[3] Benedict addresses his would-be disciples with the invitation: 'Listen to the precepts of the Master'. Therefore, as we now reflect upon his words, he would expect us to receive a wisdom which will help us as we face the problems big and small of each succeeding day.

> To you are my words now addressed, whosoever you may be,
> that, renouncing your own will to fight for the true king,
> Christ, take up the strong and glorious weapons of obedience.

St Benedict addresses us as soldiers in the army of a king! The
enemy to be defeated is, however, not a lot of other people but
the evil which can gain so easily a foothold in ourselves. It is especially, as we will later see, all those disturbing thoughts which
can, if we do not resist, invade our minds and take away our
peace. It is with this in mind that Benedict now calls us to a new
commitment. He invites us to put all our trust in Christ who,
having overcome all evil in the world, can now lead us to that
same victory, too.

> And first of all, whatever good work you undertake, ask him
> with most instant prayer to perfect it, so that he who has
> deigned to count us among his sons may never be provoked
> by our evil conduct.

Prayer takes many forms. We have already spoken quite a lot
about the communal and, therefore, structured kind which is a
celebration guided by the sentiments expressed in age-old and
inspiring texts. That is our daily liturgy. We have already mentioned, too, that silent, word-transcending form of prayer which
flows from an awareness of God's loving presence and which all
of us can have, especially, when we are calm and recollected and
at peace. What is referred to here, however, is the prayer which
rises from the ordinary circumstances of each day as we continue
on our journey through this life. We need this kind of rooted
prayer, as well. Indeed it has a very special value of its own.

This is the prayer in which we think about all that is happening
in our lives, not just because it taxes us (or fascinates us) but because we want to find in it that inner pulse which can suggest
what God himself desires us to do next! This is the prayer which,
when we see what we should do, petitions God to help us both
to do it and to do it well. This is a prayer, moreover, which can
later be infused with growing gratitude for, even as we pray, we
can become aware that God, whose word is always strong, is
promising to guide us as we do what he desires.

> For we must always so serve him with the gifts which he has given us, that he may never as an angry father disinherit his children, nor yet as a dread Lord be driven by our sins to cast into everlasting punishment the wicked servants who would not follow him to glory.

St Benedict reminds us here that, on our journey through this life, we are surrounded by a lot of people who, in different ways, may often need our help. Indeed, our true king, who is Christ, desires us to become aware of them as we continue on our way. We, therefore, could recall at this stage all that has been said already about serving others in the third part of this book. But let us note at least the veiled allusion to the Final Judgement[4] in this section of the Prologue to the Rule. It may sound rather negative but it implies that, when we have responded to the needs of others, we will be rewarded in a way which will surpass our greatest expectations and our dreams!

* * *

> Up with us then at last, for the Scripture arouses us, saying: Now is the hour for us to rise from sleep.[5] Let us open our eyes to the divine light ...

Now is the hour for us to rise from sleep! St Paul (from whom these words were taken) and the Christians of his time were under the impression that the *parousia*, the return of Christ in glory, was about to happen and they, therefore, frequently encouraged one another to 'wake up' or 'stay awake'! However, as the Lord did not return, those Christians, while remaining hopeful, had to learn to live within the confines of this often unsupportive world. St Benedict, while also looking forward to a life which is to come, exhorted his disciples to arise from sleep but his intention was that they might, thereby, see the coming of the Lord in a number of quite ordinary ways. He comes, according to the Rule, in people whom we meet, in Scripture which we can take up and read and in the intimacy of our quiet, private prayer!

> ... let us hear with attentive ears the warning that the divine voice crieth daily to us: *Today if you will hear his voice, harden*

not your hearts.[6] And again, *He that hath ears to hear, let him hear what the Spirit saith to the Churches.*[7] And what doth he say? *Come, ye children, harken unto me. I will teach you the fear of the Lord.*[8] *Run while ye have the light of life, lest the darkness of death overtake you.*[9]

'Oh, that today you would listen to his voice ...' St Benedict quotes here a psalm-verse which he would have heard each day when he and his disciples gathered for their Morning Prayer. It is a verse which, in the context of its psalm, recalls the moment when the chosen people, being weary, lost their confidence in God! At Massah in the desert they complained and did not put their trust in him who had done so much for them in the past.[10] To us, who often have our Massah moments too, this verse (which in my monastery, at least, is still heard at the start of every day) reminds us (as do all the others in the section quoted here) that God can guide and strengthen those who listen with their hearts to his all-powerful and sustaining word.

And the Lord, seeking his workman among the multitudes to whom he thus crieth, saith again, *What man is he that desireth life and would fain see good days?*[11] And if hearing him, thou answer: 'I am he', God saith to thee: *If thou wilt have true and everlasting life, keep thy tongue from evil and thy lips that they speak no guile. Turn away from evil and do good: seek after peace and pursue it.*[12]

God speaks. He does so through the verses of the psalm which is incorporated here. He tells us what we all would like to know: how to discover life and what, poetically, he refers to as, 'good days'!

The first piece of advice which God gives through the psalmist (who in this case is a sage as well!) is that we ought to keep our tongue from evil! That sounds rather negative, perhaps, but we have seen already how St Benedict, within the Rule itself, expressed his own conviction that there is a kind of talking which can harm both speaker and the spoken-to! However, we have seen as well, that he can also recommend a kind of speech which is extremely positive, indeed! He did so, for example, when he

said that, if the Cellarer has nothing else to give, he should at
least give to the one who is in need a 'good word' for, according
to the Scriptures, that is, certainly, the best gift we can give.[13] St
Benedict, no doubt, would have us all, in similar and other situations, do the same!

In any case, he says to us who seek for many things that we
should, certainly, 'seek peace'! He means not only peace with
those with whom we live (he means that too!) but also peace
within our very selves. However, let us note that this expression
'to seek peace' is similar to another one which is, moreover, central to the very purpose of the Rule.[14] This is that we 'seek God'!
There, therefore, seems to be a link between the two. Does not
the first, that peace (or *pax* to use a Benedictine word), lead us
into the mystery of God himself who is eternal peace? Indeed, is
it not also a convincing sign for those who have it that the God
whom we are seeking is already found?

'Pursue it', urged St Benedict. It is as if he knew that peace is
often difficult to find and that, when found, it can so easily disappear! 'Pursue it', said the psalmist long before and now God
says the same to each of us. Is it surprising, then, that he is looking for, not only people who are seeking him, but people who
are ready to be 'workmen', too? We have to make some kind of
effort if we wish to find that peace which comes from him.
However, let us note that in this metaphor there is, as well, the
echo of a well-known parable which tells us, if we hesitate, that
it can never be too late to start pursuing this elusive but divinely
satisfying peace.[15]

> And when you have done these things, my eyes will be upon
> you and my ears open to your prayers. And before you call
> upon me, I shall say to you: 'Lo, here I am'. What can be
> sweeter to us dearest brethren, than this voice of our Lord
> inviting us? Behold in his loving mercy the Lord showeth us
> the way of life.

This, surely, is one of the most attractive sections of the Prologue
and the Rule. It gives us one of those brief glimpses of the God to
whom St Benedict, and others like him, could respond with

warm affection and it can, if we allow it, draw us, too, into a filial relationship with him.

Within the context of the Prologue, this small section would appear to be addressed to those who have, in fact, begun to do what had been recommended to them by the psalm-verse we have seen. To them it is suggesting that the Lord, in some way, will reveal his 'loving mercy' and his kindness and himself! This is a revelation which will take place in the silence of their hearts. Moreover, it is also one which causes those who welcome it to imitate St Benedict in making their own personal commitment to the Lord. With this commitment (and with that of God to us) we will, the text implies, be able to discern more clearly how he wants us to behave on this our journey into everlasting life.

> Let us, therefore, gird our loins with faith and the perfor-
> mance of good works, and following the guidance of the
> Gospel walk in his paths, so that we may merit to see him
> who has called us into his kingdom. And if we wish to dwell
> in the tabernacle of his kingdom, except we run thither with
> good deeds, we shall not arrive.

St Benedict at this stage does not give us any details about how we ought to live. He simply indicates that, if we read the Gospels, we will find the basic guidance which we need. In doing this, however, there is something else which should be noted here! It is that he refers us not just to the Scriptures, but to one important and climactic part.

> But let us ask the Lord with the prophet: *Lord, who shall dwell
> in thy tabernacle or who shall rest upon thy holy hill?*[16] Then,
> brethren, let us hear the Lord answering and showing us the
> way that leads to that tabernacle and saying: *He that walked
> without blemish and doth what is right; he that speaketh truth in
> his heart, who hath used no deceit in his tongue, nor done evil to his
> neighbour, nor believeth ill of his neighbour.*[17] He that taketh the
> evil spirit that tempteth him, and casteth him and his tempta-
> tion from the sight of his heart, and bringeth him to naught;
> who graspeth his evil suggestions as they arise and dasheth
> them to pieces on the rock that is Christ!

St Benedict had, certainly, a weakness for the psalms! He has already in the Prologue mentioned some: the one which says that we should listen to the voice of God and, then, another which contained a mini-catalogue of how we should behave. In this brief section, he now quotes for us another two.

The first recalls what seems to have been once a dialogue between a pilgrim to Jerusalem and some wise rabbi who was telling him what he should do. The Jews, however, came to see that guidance of the rabbi as inspired and so as coming, not just from a human source, but from the Lord. St Benedict, who knew that life itself can be considered as a pilgrimage, accepts this psalm as indicating what the Lord is saying to all those who wish to make that pilgrimage each day.

The second psalm referred to in this section is not actually quoted but its final verse has been adopted as a metaphor for what we ought to do when some temptation comes. 'Be like the ruthless soldier who would dash the children of his enemy upon a nearby rock', it seems to say![18] The children of our enemy, of course, are not those people who annoy us. They are evil thoughts which can invade our minds and which, if we do not control them, can enslave and then destroy us too! Perhaps St Benedict's solution sounds dramatic but, because 'the rock is Christ',[19] to bring such thoughts to him should guarantee, not only that they will not harm us, but that any good contained in them will be preserved and, in a new and better context, be enabled to assist us as we journey on our way.

> Such men as these, fearing the Lord, are not puffed up on account of their good works, but judging that they can do no good of themselves, and that all comes from God, they magnify the Lord's work in them, using the word of the prophet: *Not unto us, O Lord, not unto us, but unto thy name give the glory.*[20] So, the apostle Paul imputed nothing of his preaching to himself, but said: *By the grace of God I am what I am.*[21] And again he saith: *He that glorieth, let him glory in the Lord.*[22]

There are times when one can feel the need to give God thanks and praise!

An interesting, historical example of such gratitude would be when Henry, king of England and his fighters overcame the French at Agincourt! According to the play of William Shakespeare, he then solemnly declared: *Let there be sung Non Nobis and Te Deum.*[23] This, which is substantiated by the records of the period, implies that those two 'hymns' must have been fairly well-known at the time. Indeed, they may have been the standard 'hymns' for such thanksgiving moments, as the latter still is to this day. However, as the Prologue testifies, the former as an isolated psalm-verse had been known, at least in certain circles, as a prayer. The early monks may not have prayed this verse with all the splendour of a later medieval choir but it may often have expressed for them a sense of deep and genuine gratitude all the same.

The gifts, however, for which we, according to the Rule, should offer thanks and praise, are more important than the winning of some war. They are the graces which we have ourselves received and which have made made it possible for us to grow as human people and, at times, enjoy much consolation, too. As Scripture says, and Benedict reminds us, it is by the grace of God that we are what we are. However there are also all the graces which have made it possible for us to help and serve our neighbour as we should. So we have many reasons to proclaim: *Not unto us, O Lord, not unto us but unto your name give the glory* and to let those sentiments become continuously ours!

* * *

Wherefore the Lord also saith in the Gospel: *He that heareth these my words and doth them, shall be likened to a wise man that built his house upon a rock. The flood came and the winds blew, and they beat upon that house, and it fell not, for it was founded upon a rock.*[24]

This, the beginning of my final section on the Prologue, reconsiders certain themes which we have seen already and which are, of course, developed in the Rule.

It starts by mentioning a well-known Gospel passage which refers to the importance both of listening to the word and of responding to the One whose word it really is. It also introduces the impressive image of the house which has been built, not on the changing sands of fashion, but on rock! This is an image of ourselves when we have let the Word of God, through daily lectio, become the sure foundation of all that we undertake and do!

It should be of some interest here to mention once again that Benedict required all those who read the word in public to be qualified. They were, in other words, to read it, whether in the church or in the refectory, in such a way that it would 'edify',[25] a word which literally means 'to build'! St Benedict, we can conclude, knew well how much the Scriptures can become, not just foundation-rock for personal stability, but also the informing element of every stage of our evolving lives!

> Having given us these instructions, the Lord daily expects us to make our life correspond with his holy admonitions. And the days of our life are lengthened and a respite allowed us for this very reason, that we may amend our evil ways. For the apostle saith: *knowest thou not that the patience of God inviteth thee to repentence?*[26] For the merciful Lord saith: *I will not the death of a sinner, but that he should be converted and live.*[27]

What seems to be considered here is, not the overall 'up-building' of our lives, but those decisive moments when we make a new commitment to the Lord. However, what St Benedict suggested when he used the 'workman' metaphor, he spells out very clearly here. It is that God, who was prepared to wait till now, is also ready to renew his invitation to us once again!

> So, brethren, we have asked the Lord about the dwellers in his tabernacle and have heard what is the duty of him who would dwell therein; it remains for us to fulfil this duty. Therefore our hearts and bodies must be made ready to fight under the holy obedience of his commands; and let us ask God that he be pleased, where our nature is powerless, to give us the help of his grace. And if we would escape the pains of hell and reach eternal life, then must we – while there is still time, while we are in this body and can fulfil all these things by the life of this light – hasten to do now what may profit us for eternity.

I have been constantly amazed at how translators of this section tend to say 'the light of life' and not the opposite which, certainly, is what the Latin *(lucis vitam)* means. I have decided, therefore, to produce my own translation here. With due respect to many scholars I have opted for *the life of light* instead.

The question which we now must ask, however, is 'what is this light to which St Benedict refers?' Is it the light to which he earlier referred and which appears to mean that insight or illumination which we can receive when we reflect upon the sacred word? It could be argued that it is.

However, even if that is the case, there is a further question to be asked. It is: 'does light mean only that or could it be suggesting something else, as well?' Does life of light not indicate the obvious, that is: a life and not just an idea? Moreover, in the context of the Prologue, does our being in that light not mean that, somehow, we are even now participating in the life which Christ already has? It surely does. Indeed, the very fact that earlier St Benedict had spoken of divine or deifying light[28] (and also of that rising out of sleep which has such Resurrection overtones) suggests that this, indeed, was what was in his mind. But, once again he has not tried to garnish or embellish such ideas but simply leaves them to us to accept with wonderment and hope.

> Therefore must we establish a school of the Lord's service, in founding which we hope to ordain nothing that is hard or burdensome.

For those for whom this Rule had been composed this 'school', of course, would have been their own monastery. Or, if the word was understood as a collective noun, the 'school' would have been all those people who were living in that place.

For those who are not monks or nuns, however, such a 'school' will be their homes or families – their parish or parishioners – or whatsoever kind of place or group it is in which they live and interact each day. Such 'schools' are most important for us all. They are the situations in which we can learn the art of serving one another and, in doing so, discover that it is, in some way which we often only glimpse, the Lord himself whom we are serving, too!

But if, for good reason, for the amendment of evil habit or the preservation of charity, there be some strictness of discipline, do not be at once dismayed and run away from the path of salvation, of which the entrance must needs be narrow.

We have here an echo of what was implied when Benedict spoke of our need to fight and, later, when he said that God was looking for a 'workman'! Serving one another can, indeed, be difficult at times! To keep it up day after day requires quite frequently a struggle, too! To do what has been recommended by the Rule, that is: what seems good, not for one's own self, but for another[29] can involve a sacrificial effort on our part! This will not mean, as we have seen, denying our essential selves but it will, certainly, demand controlling our more superficial and unanchored selves so that we may both grow and blossom as we should.

> But, as we progress in our monastic life and in faith, our hearts shall be enlarged, and we shall run with unspeakable sweetness of love in the way of God's commandments.

This is, certainly, one of the most encouraging assertions in the Rule. It is, moreover, one of those parts of the Prologue which has not been taken from the same source as the rest and which was, possibly, composed by the author of the Rule himself. It does, however (as we must admit) refer directly to monastic life but what it says can be applied to other forms of Christian living, too. Do not the very Gospels speak about a joy which is complete?[30] As for the running does it not suggest a great enthusiasm which we all can have for, even as a word, it signifies the movement of God's Spirit in our lives.[31]

> So that, never abandoning his Rule, but persevering in his teaching in the monastery until death, we shall share by patience in the sufferings of Christ, that we may deserve to be partakers also of his kingdom. Amen.

Change 'monastery' for whatsoever group it is to which you are yourself committed. Take and hold on to the essence of the Rule if you have found that it provides the basic framework which you need and, like the Benedictine monks and nuns of this and every age, allow those passages which help you to keep flowing through your mind. The attitudes which they enshrine will then begin to mould your own and give a new and a distinctive flavour to your lives.

One final, but important, thought! It is that, on our journey through this life, we are united in the Spirit to the one who leads us, who is Christ. But he is not just one particular individual, however great. He is a universal and inclusive person in whom all of us, who follow him, exist.[32] Our sufferings are, therefore, somehow his while, on the other hand, our patience will allow his triumph to be ours! There is a mystery in this and it is one to which the final sentence of the Prologue provocatively points.

Notes

PART ONE

Benedict himself

1. Pope St Gregory the Great (540-604) composedthe *Dialogues*, Book Two of which contains the legends of St Benedict, though presented in St Gregory's own way.

2. David Knowles writing on *The Benedictine Tradition in Europe*, says: *For many centuries almost all the writers and very many of the most distinguisghed bishops and royal councillors and administrators had heard every day, year in and year out, a section of the Rule read in Chapter, and as novices had learnt it by heart as a guide for their lives.* (Published in *A Vision of Europe* by the Cathedral Church of St Michael, Coventry. 1967)

3. *Fulgens Radiator*, the Encyclical letter of Pius XII, issued on the occasion of the 14th centenary of the death of Benedict. cf. A.A.S. (1947) p 453.

4. The papal Brief, *Pacis Nunctius* of Paul VI was issued on the 24th Oct 1964. The qualification 'all' was to include the eastern countries which, at that time, were within the Soviet block.

5. cf. Homily of Pope John Paul II at Nursia on 23rd March 1980.

6. *The Life of Benedict* by Gregory the Great, translated by Pearce Cusack, O.Cist. Published by Carmelite Centre of Spirituality (Ireland) 1980, p 19.

7. Rule of Benedict, chapter four.

8. Life of Benedict, op.cit. p19.

9. cf. Rule of Benedict, Prologue & chapter 61, and 2 Tim 2:4.

10. Life of Benedict, op.cit. p 20.

11. Rule of Benedict, chapter 1.

l2. Life of Benedict, op.cit. pp 21-22.

13. Life of Benedict, cf. op.cit. p 22. (NB. I have used de Vogüé's translation here, St.Bede's publications, Massachusetts. 1993)

14 Life of Benedict, op.cit. p.26.

The Rule

1. St.Gregory in the Dialogues wrote: *He wrote a Rule for Monks which is remarkable both for its discretion and for the lucidity of its style. If anyone wishes to know his character and life more precisely, he may find in the ordinances of the Rule a complete account of the abbot's practice for the holy man*

cannot have taught otherwise than as he lived. Life of Benedict, op.cit. pp 55-56.

2. *The Rule of Benedict as a guide for Christian Living* by Harald Schtzeichel, *American Benedictine Review,* June 1988, p 190.

3. The Rule of the Master is a 6th century document about three times as long as the Rule of Benedict. For a long time it was presumed to be a somewhat tedious expansion of St Benedict's Rule but now the scholars are agreed that it is, certainly, the earlier of the two.

4. Saints Augustine (354-430) & Basil(c.329-379) were early Bishops and Doctors of the Church. John Cassian (c.360-c.435) was a monk at Bethlehem who visited the old monastic settlements in Egypt, then travelled on to Gaul where, near Marseilles, he founded two monastic houses, one for men and one for women.

5. Life of Benedict, op.cit. pp 44-45.

6. *Living with Contradictions* by Esther de Waal, Collins (1989) p 41.

7. Rule of Benedict, chapter 22.

8. Rule of Benedict, chapter 36.

9. Rule of Benedict, chapter 39.

10 cf. Rule of Benedict, chapter 2.

11. cf. Rule of Benedict, chapter 64.

12. Rule of Benedict, chapter 31.

PART TWO

A Balanced Way of Life

1. The Rule of Benedict, chapter 16, refers to seven offices each day and one which takes place in the night. A lot of monasteries today, however, have reduced this to a Morning and an Evening Prayer, one Midday Hour, a Night Prayer and, on certain days, a longer Vigil Office. The Church's 'Daily Praye' (the Roman Breviary) has much the same.

2. Rule of Benedict, chapter 48. The sentence has been quoted from the Rule of St Basil.

3. cf. *Ora et Labora: Devise Benedictine* by Soeur Marie-Benoit Meeuws, OSB, *Collectanea Cisterciensia* 54,1992-3.

4. Lk 10:38-42. Some commentators like to link this passage with Acts 6:1-6. The early Church authorities discovered that to serve the needy takes a lot of time and energy and so, in order to have time for prayer as well, they spread the burden of the work.

5. Maurus Wolter (1825-1890) was a German who had joined the Benedictine Abbey of St Paul's-outside-the-walls, in Rome. In 1860 he returned to Germany and founded there a monastery at Beuron. As its abbot he became a strong promoter of the liturgy and of that form of painting which was later known as Beuronese. His abbey prospered and made quite a number of foundations throughout Germany and Belgium in the last part of his century.

6. Rule of Benedict, chapter 43.

7. Rule of Benedict, chapter 48.
8. Rule of Benedict, chapter 66.
9. cf. *Living with Contradiction* by Esther de Waal, Collins (1989)p 40.
10. 2 Cor 4:16-18.

Lectio Divina
1. St Benedict 'is far more discerning than any of his predecessors in allocating the time for reading to those periods of the day, especially in the morning, which are physically more congenial for that exercise.'
Consider Your Call: A Theology of Monastic Life by Daniel Rees & others, SPCK (1978)p 264.
2. 'Book' in English comes from the Greek word: *Biblios*.
3. Rule of Benedict, chapter 73.
4. *Decree on Divine Revelation*, no.21, Costello Publishing Company, N.Y. (1975) p 762.
5. *The Phrase 'lectio divina' began its career as an equivalent to 'sacra pagina' when that name was used to describe the objective text of the lessons in liturgical worship.*
Consider Your Call, SPCK (1978) p 265.
6. *The Love of Learning and the Desire for God* by Jean Leclercq, OSB. SPCK (1974) p 89.
7. 'Murmuring' in the Rule refers to grumbling which is generally thought to be unreasonable and destructive of community, as well.
8. *Lectio Divina and the Monastic Spirituality of Reading*, by Monica Sandor, The American Benedictine Review, 40:1-March 1989, p 97.
9. cf. Rev.10:8-10
10. *Lectio Divina and the Monastic Spirituality of Reading*, by Monica Sandor, The American Benedictine Review, 40:1-March 1989, p 97. cf. Pss.18/19,10; 33/34,8.
11. A good example would be the Summa Theologica of St Thomas Aquinas.
12. Guigo (+1188) was a Carthusian monk and 9th Prior of La Grande Chartreuse in France. The short treatise known to us as The Ladder for Monks has been attributed to him.
13. The Ladder for Monks by Guigo, translated by Edmund Colledge, OSA & James Walsh SJ, Image Books, NY (1978), p 83.
14. ibid. p 87.
15. Columba Marmion (1858-1923) joined the monastery of Maredsous and was, in 1909, elected as its abbot. He was one of the great spiritual Masters of his age and, basing much of what he said on Scripture, he prepared the way for others to develop the more biblically-grounded spirituality which is popular today.
16. From a letter of Marmion, dated 9/8/1920. cf *Abbot Columba Marmion* by Dom Raymund Thibaut. Sands & Co (1932) p 451.
17. cf. Rule of Benedict, chapter 48.
18. *Monastic Lectio: Some Clues from Terminology* by Ambrose Wathen OSB, *Monastic Studies* 12(1976), p 215.

Prayer
1. Rule of Benedict, chapter 53.
2. cf. Gen 1:2. The Hebrew word for this confused material was 'tohubohu'.
3. cf. Gen 1:26. The Word of God makes humankind, and makes it in his image and his likeness.
4. Mt 18:20.
5. Rom 12:5.
6. ibid. cf. 1 Cor 12:12-26.
7. Ps 69/70,1. For liturgical use this verse, which in the psalm is singular, is given in the plural form.
8. cf. Ps 79/80.
9. cf. Pss 45/46; 47/48; 86/87.
10. cf. Pss 120/121; 121/122; 123/124; 127/128; 129/130; 130/131.
11. cf. Pss 22/23; 76/77; 77/78.
12. cf. Pss 19/20; 20/21; 71/72; 95/96; 96/97; 97/98; 98/99.
13. Lamentation psalms are numerous but special mention could be made of Pss 21/22 & 68/69.
14. cf. Pss 33/34; 148; 150.
15. Rule of Benedict, chapter 58.
16. Rule of Benedict, chapter 8.
17. Rule of Benedict, chapter 48.
18. Rule of Benedict, chapter 19.

Commitment
1. Rule of Benedict, chapter 58.
2. ibid.
3. Life of Benedict, op.cit. p 58 (*Dialogues*, Bk 3, chapter 16).
4. Eph. 3:17
5. Rule of Benedict, chapter 58. (translation mine)
6. Rule of Benedict, chapter 73. (translation mine)
7. Rule of Benedict, chapter 62. (translation mine)
8. Rule of Benedict, chapter 6. (quotation from 2 Cor 9:7)
9. Rule of Benedict, chapter 58.
10. The basis for this formula is the verse in chapter 58 of the Rule which declares: *In the Oratory, in the presence of all, he shall promise stability, conversion of his life and obedience.* Unlike the medieval vows which separated the 'religious' from the ordinary laity, these vows concern what is essential for the lives of all.

Overflow
1. Life of Benedict, op.cit.p 22.
2. Life of Benedict, op.cit.p 56.
3. Rule of Benedict, chapter 64.
4. Rule of Benedict, chapter 2. (italics mine)
5. *On the song of Songs* by Bernard of Clairvaux, Sermon 18,1,3, Cistercian Publications Inc.,Kalamazoo, Michegan 49008, (1979), p 134.

6. Aelred of Rievaulx (1110-1167). Born in Northumberland, he joined the Cistercian Abbey at Rievaulx and, in time, became its Abbot. He was known as 'the Bernard of the North'.

7. *The Mirror of Charity* by Aelred of Rievaulx, A.R.Mowbray & Co.Ltd, London (1962), p 85.

8. Life of Benedict, op.cit.p 32.

9. Lk 1:41.

PART THREE

The Garden Shed

1. Rule of Benedict, chapter 4.

2. Mt 22:34-40.

3. Chapters 4-7 of the Rule of Benedict is called 'the Spiritual Directory' by the Benedictine scholar, Adalbert de Vogüé.

4. Rule of Benedict, chapter 7.

5. The commandment 'Honour your father and your mother' has been changed to 'honour all' as being more appropriate for those who, having left their families, now practice open hospitality.

6. Rule of Benedict, chapter 4.

7. Mt 7:12. cf.Tobit 4:15.

8. St.Benedict shows his concern for individuals when speaking about what the monks should eat, when speaking about those who are overburdened in their work and when referring to those who are overcome with sorrow, even though they may have brought it on themselves.

9. cf. Rule of Benedict, chapter 2.

10. Rule of Benedict, chapter 4.

11. ibid.

12. ibid.

13. ibid.

14. ibid.

15. ibid.

16. ibid.

17. Benedict moved to Monte Cassino because a local priest at Subiaco was attempting to destroy the communities which he was building there. While Benedict was still not far away that priest fell from the balcony of his house and died. Far from being mightily relieved, however, Benedict *lamented bitterly, both for the death of his enemy and because his disciple (who had told him) had exulted in it.* Life of Benedict, op.cit. p 31.

18. Rule of Benedict, chapter 4.

19. ibid.

20. cf. Acts.17:28.

21. Rule of Benedict, chapter 4.

The Ballet
1. Rule of Benedict, chapter 35.
2. ibid.
3. Rule of Benedict, chapter 38.
4. Rule of Benedict, chapter 35.
5. Rule of Benedict, chapter 72.
6. Rule of Benedict, chapter 35.
7. Rule of Benedict, chapter 72.
8. Rule of Benedict, chapter 35.
9. Life of Benedict, op.cit. p 41-42. *One evening, when the venerable man was at his supper a monk of a distinguished family was holding a light for him by the table. And while the man of God ate his meal and the other stood there with the lamp, the spirit of pride entered into the monk and he began secretly to ponder such thoughts as these: 'Who is this man that I am waiting on as he eats, serving him and holding a light for him?*
10. Rule of Benedict, chapter 35.
11. ibid.
12. Rule of Benedict, chapter 4.
13. Acts 2:46-47.
14. Rule of Benedict, chapters 38, 63.
15. Rule of Benedict, chapters 60, 61, 62.
16. *Receiving Communion – A Forgotten Symbol* by Robert Taft, *Worship* Vol.57; Sept. 1983.

Fine-tuning
1. Rule of Benedict, chapter 31.
2. Rule of Benedict, chapter 35.
3. This section of the Rule of Benedict is not found in its major source: the Rule of the Master.
4. Rule of Benedict, chapter 37.
5. ibid.
6. Rule of Benedict, chapter 36.
7. ibid.
8. ibid.
9. ibid.
10. ibid.
11. ibid.
12. i.e. The Rule of the Master.
13. Rule of Benedict, chapter 53.
14. Rule of Benedict, chapter 66.
15. Life of Benedict, op.cit. p 48.
16. Rule of Benedict, chapter 4.
17. cf. Gen 1:31.
18. Rule of Benedict, chapter 36.
19. Rule of Benedict, chapter 53.
20. Rule of Benedict, chapter 2.

The Dream
1. Rule of Benedict, chapter 33. (cf Acts 4:32). This sentence was not in the Rule of the Master.
2. Acts 2:44. cf. 4:32. This sentence was not in the Rule of the Master.
3. cf. Rule of Benedict, chapters 39, 40, 55.
4. Exod 16:18.
5. Rule of Benedict, chapter 34.
6. Acts 5:1-11.
7. Acts 6:1-6.
8. Rule of Benedict, chapter 57.
9. Rule of Benedict, chapter 72.
10. Rule of Benedict, chapter 7.
11. Rule of Benedict, chapter 4.
12. Rule of Benedict, chapter 72.
13. Rule of Benedict, chapter 71.
14. Rule of Benedict, chapter 72.
15. Abram became Abraham the father of many (Gen 17:5); Jacob became Israel because he struggled with God (Gen 32:28); and Simon became Peter for he was, in spite of all his weaknesses, a rock. (Jn 1:42).
16. Rom 8:28.

A Hospital of Sorts!
1. Rule of Benedict, chapter 43.
2. Rule of Benedict, chapter 46.
3. Rule of Benedict, chapter 71.
4. cf. Rule of Benedict, chapter 4.
5. Eph 4:16.
6. Rule of Benedict, chapter 11.
7. Rule of Benedict, chapter 46.
8. Rule of Benedict, chapter 1.
9. Rule of Benedict, chapter 28.
10. ibid.
11. Rule of Benedict, chapter 13.
12. ibid.
13. Heb 12:22.

Patientia!
1. 1 Pet 4:13.
2. Rule of Benedict, chapter 49.
3. ibid.
4. Rule of Benedict, chapter 4.
5. Life of Benedict, op.cit. p 30-31.
6. Rule of Benedict, chapter 36.
7. ibid.
8. Rule of Benedict, chapter 72.
9. Infirmitates suas! 'Suas', unlike 'eius', has a reflexive connotation. Italics mine.

PART FOUR

Awareness
1. Rule of Benedict, chapter 19.
2. cf. Rule of Benedict, chapters 2, 36, 53.
3. Rule of Benedict, chapter 4.
4. *Ever Present Lord* by Bishop Joseph Gerry, OSB, St Bede's Publications (1989) p 4.
5. Life of Benedict, op.cit. p 21.
6. Rule of Benedict, chapter 57.
7. Rule of Benedict, chapter 31.
8. cf Wis 13:5; Rom 1:20.

Responsive Listening
1. Rule of Benedict, chapter 6.
2. Rule of Benedict, chapter 3.
3. Sir (Ecclus) 32:24.
4. cf. Jas 1:17.
5. cf. Rule of Benedict, chapter 1.
6. Rule of Benedict, chapter 7.
7. Rule of Benedict, chapter 46.
8. Rule of Benedict, chapter 4.
9. Rule of Benedict, chapter 49.
10. Rule of Benedict, chapter 48.
11. ibid.
12. This Ladder-metaphor had been already used by Cassian and the Master.
13. 'A wise-man is known by the fewness of his words.' Rule of Benedict, chapter 7.
14. Rule of Benedict, chapter 6.
15. Rule of Benedict, chapter 7.
16. We read in the beginning of chapter seven in the Rule: *Wherefore, brethren, if we wish to attain to the summit of humility and desire to arrive speedily at that heavenly exaltation to which we ascend by humility of the present life, then must we set up a ladder of our ascending actions like unto that which Jacob saw in his vision, whereupon angels appeared to him, descending and ascending. By that descent and ascent we must surely understand nothing else than this, that we descend by self-exaltation and ascend by humility.*
17. Rule of Benedict, chapter 7.
18. ibid.
19. ibid.
20. Life of Benedict, op.cit. pp 52-53.

Contentment
1. Rule of Benedict, chapter 61. Perhaps these unconnected monks were not unlike those Christians of today who, though committed, have not

found a guiding and supportive group.
2. ibid.
3. Rule of Benedict, chapter 7.
4. Rule of Benedict, chapter 53.
5. Rule of Benedict, chapter 7.
6. ibid.
7. Rule of Benedict, chapter 62.
8. cf. Acts 17:28

PART FIVE

Back to the Beginning!
1. i.e. The Rule of the Master.
2. i.e. the Rule of the Master.
3. Prov 1:8. cf also 3:1; 4:1-20; 5:1; 6:20.
4. cf. Mt 25:31-46.
5. Rom 13:11.
6. Ps 94/95.
7. Mt 11:15; Rev 2:7.
8. Ps 33/34.
9. Jn 12:35.
10. Exod 17:1-7.
11. Ps 33/34.
12. ibid.
13. Rule of Benedict, chapter 31; Ecclus 18:17.
14. Rule of Benedict, chapter 58.
15. Mt 20:1-16.
16. Ps 14/15.
17. ibid.
18. Ps 136/137.
19. cf. 1 Cor 10:4. According to a Jewish tradition, the rock in the desert from which water came acccompanied the Israelites on their journey to the Promised Land.
20 Ps 113/115.
21. 1 Cor 15:10.
22. 2 Cor 10:17.
23. A quotation from Henry V in Shakespeare's play of that same name. Historical records testify that: *the king gathering his armie together gave thanks to almightie God for so happie a victorie, causing his prelats and chaplains to sing this psalm and commanded everie man to kneele down on the ground at this verse: 'Non nobis, Domine, non nobis, sed nomini tuo da gloriam'. King Henry the Fifth, Poet Historical* by W.F.P.Stockley, Heath Cranton Ltd 1925, p 104.
24. Mt 7:24-27.
25. Rule of Benedict, chapters 38 & 47. (cf also chapters 42 & 53)

26. Rom 2:4.
27. Ez 18:23.
28. *deificum* is often translated as divine but the word itself contains the thought of divinising.
29. Rule of Benedict, chapter 72.
30. Jn 15:11.
31. *Enthusiasm* as a word is made up of the Greek for 'God' *(theos)* and the preposition 'in' *(en)*!
32. cf. Col 1:17.